The International Behavioural and Social Sciences Library

THE CHILD AND THE FAMILY

TAVISTOCK

FAMILIES & MARRIAGE
In 6 Volumes

I	Family and Social Network *Elizabeth Bott*
II	Motherhood and Personality *Léon Chertok*
III	Family Influences and Psychosomatic Illness *E M Goldberg*
IV	Family Ill Health *Robert Kellner*
V	Neurosis in the Ordinary Family *Anthony Ryle*
VI	The Child and the Family *D W Winnicott*

THE CHILD AND THE FAMILY

First Relationships

D W WINNICOTT

Routledge
Taylor & Francis Group
LONDON AND NEW YORK

First published in 1957 by
Tavistock Publications Limited

Reprinted in 2001 by
Routledge
2 Park Square, Milton Park, Abingdon, Oxon, OX14 4RN

711 Third Avenue, New York, NY 10017

Transferred to Digital Printing 2007

Routledge is an imprint of the Taylor & Francis Group

First issued in paperback 2013

The publishers have made every effort to contact authors/copyright holders of the works reprinted in the *International Behavioural and Social Sciences Library*. This has not been possible in every case, however, and we would welcome correspondence from those individuals/companies we have been unable to trace.

These reprints are taken from original copies of each book. In many cases the condition of these originals is not perfect. The publisher has gone to great lengths to ensure the quality of these reprints, but wishes to point out that certain characteristics of the original copies will, of necessity, be apparent in reprints thereof.

British Library Cataloguing in Publication Data
A CIP catalogue record for this book
is available from the British Library

The Child and the Family
ISBN 13 978-0-415-26422-8 (Hardback)
ISBN 13 978-0-415-84639-4 (Paperback)

Families & Marriage: 6 Volumes
ISBN 0-415-26508-8
The International Behavioural and Social Sciences Library
112 Volumes
ISBN 0-415-25670-4

D. W. WINNICOTT

The Child and the Family

First Relationships

EDITED BY

JANET HARDENBERG
M.B.

TAVISTOCK PUBLICATIONS LTD

First published in 1957
by Tavistock Publications Limited
2 Park Square, Milton Park, Abingdon, Oxon, OX14 4RN

Second impression 1962

in 11-point Baskerville by
Bradford & Dickens, London

EDITOR'S NOTE

Dr. Winnicott has, during the past eighteen years or so, written and broadcast on various aspects of the theory and practice of child care. There have been numerous requests that the papers and talks should be brought together in a book, and my task has been to arrange and edit them for publication in this form.

It seemed best, in the first place, to arrange the papers according to subject matter, and not in chronological order. This has led to a natural grouping in two volumes: one containing, in the main, broadcast talks to parents about their infants and very young children, with a few particularly relevant additional papers; the other comprising talks to teachers, social workers, and those who have the care of children not their own. Certain subjects are common to both groups—for example, stealing and telling lies, and breast feeding—and they are discussed from different aspects.

I have made only minor alterations to the original papers, preferring a certain amount of repetition to too much dislocation of the text. Wherever possible, the date and source of first publication or broadcast have been given. This volume contains Dr. Winnicott's talks to parents, which attempt to link new knowledge and theory with the natural wisdom of fathers and mothers, and from them emerges what is almost a meditation on the nature of normal family life.

JANET HARDENBERG, M.B.

ACKNOWLEDGMENTS

Thanks are recorded to the following individuals and organisations for permission to publish material that has already appeared in print: the British Broadcasting Corporation; the Editors of *Young Children;* and the Editor of the *New Era in Home and School,* who has been particularly kind and helpful over matters of detail.

PREFACE

THESE direct talks to parents, given mostly in the period 1940–50, are now collected together, without appreciable alteration.

Always an author owes a great deal to audiences, and I more than most. The great stimulus for me was Miss Janet Quigley's proposal during the war years that I should give a series of weekly broadcasts to mothers. Of this first series a few appeared in a pamphlet called *Getting to Know Your Baby,* now out of print. A new stimulus came in 1949 from Miss I. D. Benzie (Mrs. Royston Morley) who was the producer for eleven more B.B.C. talks, nine of which appeared in a pamphlet called *The Ordinary Devoted Mother and Her Baby* (now also out of print).

It was Dr. Peggy Volkov, who has for many years been Editor of the *New Era in Home and School,* who first persuaded me to get talks to parent groups down on paper, and I shall always be grateful to her for her encouragement.

The many others who have helped me shall be nameless. I can only hope that I, in turn, have helped them.

D. W. WINNICOTT
F.R.C.P. (LOND.)

CONTENTS

Contents

PART I

The Ordinary Devoted Mother and her Baby

1

A Man Looks at Motherhood

[1949]

To begin with, you will be relieved to know that I am not going to be telling you what to do. I am a man, and so I can never really know what it is like to see wrapped up over there in the cot a bit of my own self, a bit of me living an independent life, yet at the same time dependent and gradually becoming a person. Only a woman can experience this, and perhaps only a woman can imaginatively experience it, as she has to do when by bad luck of one kind or another the actual experience is lacking.

What is there for me to do, then, if I am not going to give instructions? I'm used to having mothers bring their children to me, and when this happens we see what we want to talk about right before our eyes. The baby is jumping about on the mother's knee, reaching out for things on my desk, climbing down on to the floor and crawling round; clambering up on the chairs, or pulling books out of the book-cases; or perhaps clinging to mother in dread of the white-coated doctor who will surely be a monster who eats children if they are nice, and who does worse things if they are nasty. Or an older child is at a separate table drawing pictures while mother and I are trying to piece together the history of his development, and trying to see where things started to go wrong. The child is listening out of one ear to make sure we are up to no mischief, and at the same time is communicating with me without speaking, by the drawings which I go over to see from time to time.

How easy is all this, and how different is my task now, when I have to build baby and small child out of my imagination and experience!

You have had the same difficulty. If I cannot communicate with you, what did you feel like having a baby a few weeks old, not knowing what was, or was not, there to communicate with? If you are thinking this out, try to remember at what age your baby or babies seemed to notice you as a person, and what made you feel fairly sure at that exciting moment that you were two people communicating with each other. You did not have to do everything from different sides of the room, by talking. What language would you have used? No, you found yourself concerned with management of the baby's body, and you liked it to be so. You knew just how to pick the baby up, how to put the baby down, and how to leave well alone, letting the cot act for you; and you had learnt how to arrange the clothes for comfort and for preserving the baby's natural warmth. Indeed, you knew all this when you were a little girl and played with dolls. And then there were special times when you did definite things, feeding, bathing, changing napkins, and cuddling. Sometimes the urine trickled down your apron or went right through and soaked you as if you yourself had let slip, and you didn't mind. In fact by these things you could have known that you were a woman, and an ordinary devoted mother.

I am saying all this because I want you to know that this man, nicely detached from real life, free from the noise and smell and responsibility of child care, does know that the mother of a baby is tasting real things, and that she would not miss the experience for worlds. If we understand each other thus far, you will perhaps let me talk about being an ordinary devoted mother and managing the earliest stages of the life of a new human being. I cannot tell you exactly what to do, but I can talk about what it all means.

In the ordinary things you do you are quite naturally doing very important things, and the beauty of it is that you do not have to be clever, and you do not even have to think if you do not want to. You may have been hopeless at arithmetic at school, or perhaps all your friends got scholarships, but you didn't like the sight of a history book, and so failed and left school early; or perhaps you would have done well if you hadn't had measles just before the exam. Or you may be really clever. But all this does not matter, and it hasn't anything to do with whether you are a good mother or not. If a child can play with a doll, you can be an ordinary devoted mother, and I believe you are just this most of the time.

Isn't it strange that such a tremendously important thing should depend so little on exceptional intelligence!

If human babies are to develop eventually into healthy, independent, and society-minded adult individuals, they absolutely depend on being given a good start, and this good start is assured in nature by the existence of the bond between the baby's mother and the baby, the thing called love. So if you love your baby he or she is getting a good start.

Let me quickly say that I am not talking about sentimentality. You all know the kind of person who goes about saying, 'I simply *adore* babies'. But you wonder, do they love them? A mother's love is a pretty crude affair. There's possessiveness in it, appetite, even a 'drat the kid' element; there's generosity in it, and power, as well as humility. But sentimentality is outside it altogether, and is repugnant to mothers.

Now, it may be that you are an ordinary devoted mother, and you like being one without thinking about it. Artists are often the very people who hate thinking about art, and about the purpose of art. You, as a mother, may prefer to avoid thinking things out, so I want to warn you that in this book we are going to talk about the things a devoted mother does by just being herself. But a few will like to consider what they are doing. Probably some of you have finished with actual mothering, and your children have grown up and gone to school; you may then like to look back on the good things you did, and think about the way in which you laid the foundation for your children's development. If you did it all intuitively, probably that was the best way.

It is vitally important that we should get to understand the part played by those who care for the infant, so that we can protect the young mother from whatever tends to get between herself and her child. If she is without understanding of the thing she does so well she is without means to defend her position, and only too easily she spoils her job by trying to do what she is told, or what her own mother did, or what the books say.

Fathers come into this, not only by the fact that they can be good mothers for limited periods of time, but also because they can help to protect the mother and baby from whatever tends to interfere with the bond between them, which is the essence and very nature of child care.

In the following talks I shall be deliberately trying to put into words what a mother does when she is ordinarily and quite simply devoted to her baby.

We still have much to learn about infants at the beginning, and only mothers can tell us what we want to know. Babies differ from each other enormously, and neither early nor late development will show us whether or not the child is going to be a Cabinet Minister!

2

Getting to Know Your Baby

[1944]

A WOMAN's life changes in many ways when she conceives a child. Up to this point she may have been a person of wide interests, perhaps in business, or a keen politician, or an enthusiastic tennis player, or one who has always been ready for a dance or a 'do'. She may have tended to despise the relatively restricted lives of friends who have had a child, making rude remarks about their resemblance to vegetables. She may have been actually repelled by such technical details as the washing and airing of napkins. If she has been interested in children, her interest can be said to have been sentimental rather than practical. But sooner or later she herself becomes pregnant.

At first it may easily happen that she resents this fact, because she can see only too clearly what a terrible interference with her 'own' life it must mean. What she sees is true enough, and it would be silly for any one to deny it. Babies are a lot of trouble, and they are a positive nuisance unless they are wanted. If a young woman has not yet begun to want the baby she is carrying she cannot avoid feeling that she is just unlucky.

Experience shows, however, that a change gradually takes place in the feelings as well as in the body of the girl who has conceived. Shall I say her interest gradually narrows down? Perhaps it is better to say that the direction of her interest turns from outwards to inwards. She slowly but surely comes to believe that the centre of the world is in her own body.

Perhaps some reader has just arrived at this stage, and is beginning to feel a little proud of herself, to feel she is someone who deserves respect, and for whom people should naturally make way on the pavement.

As you become more and more sure that you will soon become a mother you begin to put all your eggs into one basket, as the saying is. You begin to take the risk of allowing yourself to be concerned with one object, the little boy or girl human being that will be born. This little boy or girl will be yours in the deepest possible sense, and you will be his or hers.

To become a mother you go through a great deal, and I think that it is because you go through so much that you become able to see with especial clearness certain fundamental principles of infant care, so that it takes years of study for those who are not mothers to get as far in understanding as you may get in the ordinary course of your experience. But you may very well need support from those of us who study you, because superstitions and old wives' tales —some of them quite modern ones—come along and make you doubt your own true feelings.

Let us consider just what it is that the ordinary healthy-minded mother knows about her baby that is so vitally important, and yet which is apt to be forgotten by those who only look on. I think the most important thing is that you easily feel that your baby is worth getting to know as a person, and worth getting to know from the earliest possible moment. No one who comes along to give you advice will ever know this as well as you know it yourself.

Even in the womb your baby is a human being, unlike any other human being, and by the time he is born he will have had quite a lot of experience, unpleasant as well as pleasant. It is, of course, easy to read into the face of a new-born baby things that are not there; though to be sure, a baby may look very wise at times, even philosophical. But if I were you I should not wait until the psychologists have decided how human a baby is at birth—I should just go right ahead and get to know the little fellow, and let him get to know you.

You already know something of your baby's characteristics because of the movements you have learned to expect from him inside your womb. If there has been a lot of movement you have wondered how much there is in the amusing saying that boys kick more than girls do; and in any case you have been pleased to have the actual sign of life and liveliness that this quickening has provided. And during this time the baby has, I suppose, come to know quite a lot about you. He has shared your meals. His blood has flowed more quickly when you drank a nice cup of tea in the morning, or when you ran to catch a bus. To some extent he must have known whenever you were anxious or excited or angry. If you have been restless he has become used to movement, and he may expect to be jogged on your knee or rocked in his cradle. If, on the other hand, you are a restful sort of person he has known peace, and may expect a quiet lap and a still pram. In a way I should say that he knows you better than you know him, until he is born, and you hear his cry, and are well enough to look at him, and to take him in your arms.

Babies and mothers vary tremendously in their condition after the event of birth, and perhaps it will be two or three days in your case before you and your baby are both fit to enjoy each other's company. But there is no real reason why you shouldn't start to get to know each other right away, if you are well enough. I know a young mother who made a very early contact with her baby boy, her first child. From the day of his birth, after each feed, he was put in a cradle and left by his mother's bed by the sensible matron of the nursing home. For a while he would lie awake in the quiet of the room, and the mother would put down her hand to him; and before he was a week old he began to catch hold of her fingers and look up in her direction. This intimate relationship continued without interruption and developed, and I believe it has helped to lay the foundation for the child's personality and for what we call his emotional development, and his capacity to withstand the frustrations and shocks that sooner or later came his way.

The most impressive part of your early contact with your baby will be at his feed-times, that is to say, when he is excited. You may be excited too, and you may be having feelings in your breasts which indicate that you are usefully excited, and that you are preparing to give milk. The baby is fortunate if he can take you and your excitements for granted at first, so that he can get on with the business of meeting and managing his own impulses and urges. For, according to my view, it is a most alarming thing to be an infant discovering the feelings that turn up when excitement comes along. Have you ever looked at it in that way?

You will see from this that you have to get to know your infant in two states, when he is contented, and more or less unexcited, and when he is excited. At first, when he is unexcited, he will spend a great deal of his time asleep, but not all his time, and the moments of waking but peaceful life are precious. I know that some babies hardly ever manage to get satisfied and for a long time cry and show distress, even after feeding, and do not sleep easily, and in this case it is very difficult for the mother to make satisfactory contact. But in time things will probably settle down, and there will be some contentment, and perhaps during the bath-time there will be a chance for the beginnings of a human relationship.

One reason why you should get to know your baby both in contentment and in excitement is that he needs your help. And you cannot give this help unless you know where you are with him. He needs you to help him to manage the awful transitions from sleeping or waking contentment to all-out greedy attack. This could be said to be your first task as a mother, apart from routine, and a lot of skill is required which only the child's mother can possess, unless it be some good woman who adopts a baby in the first days after birth.

For instance, babies are not born with an alarum clock hanging round their necks, with instructions: feed three-hourly. Regular feeding is a convenience to the mother or to the nurse, and from the baby's point of view it may well turn out that regular feeding is the next best thing to having a pull whenever the impulse to feed turns up. But a baby does not necessarily start off *wanting* regular feeds; in fact, I think that what an infant expects to find is a breast that comes as it is wanted and disappears as it is unwanted. Occasionally a mother may have to give her breast in a gipsy way for a short period of time before she can adopt a rigid routine that suits her convenience. At any rate, it is well that when you are getting to know your baby you should know what it is that he starts off expecting, even if you decide that he cannot have it. And, if you know the whole of your infant, you will find that it is only when he is excited that he has such an imperious nature. In between times he is only too glad to find mother behind the breast or bottle, and to find the room behind mother, and the world outside the room. Whereas there is a tremendous amount to learn about your baby during his feed times, you will see that I am suggesting that there is even more to learn about him while he is in his bath, or lying in his cot, or when you are changing his napkins.

If you are being looked after by a nurse, I hope she will understand me and not feel I am interfering when I say that you are at a disadvantage if your baby is only handed to you at feed-times. You need nurse's help, and you are not yet strong enough to top and tail the baby yourself. But if you do not know your sleeping baby, or your baby as he lies awake wondering, you must get a very funny impression of him when he is handed to you just for you to feed him. At this time he is a bundle of discontent, a human being to be sure, but one who has raging lions and tigers inside him. And he is almost certainly scared by his own feelings. If no one has explained all this to you, you may become scared too.

If, on the other hand, you already know your infant by watching him as he lies by your side, and by allowing him to play in your arms, and at your breast, you will see his excitement in its proper proportions and recognise it as a form of love. You will also be in a position to understand what is happening when he turns his head away and refuses to drink, like the proverbial horse taken to the water, or when he goes to sleep in your arms instead of working at his feed, or when he becomes agitated so that he is no good at his job. He is just scared of his own feelings, and you can help him at this point as no one else can by your great patience, and by allowing play, by allowing him to mouth the nipple, perhaps to handle it; anything that the infant can let himself enjoy, till at last he gains the confidence to take the risk and suck. This is not easy for you, because you have yourself to think of too, your breasts being either over-full or else waiting till the baby sucks before beginning to fill. But if you know what is happening you will be able to tide over the difficult time, and enable your baby to establish a good relation to you when he feeds.

He is not so silly, either. When you think that excitement means an experience for him rather like what being put in a den of lions would be for us, no wonder he wants to make sure you are a reliable milk-giver before he lets himself go for you. If you fail him it must feel to him as if the wild beasts will gobble him up. Give him time and he will discover you, and you will both eventually come to value even his greedy love of your breasts.

I think that an important thing about a young mother's experience of *early* contact with her baby is the reassurance that it gives her that her child is normal (whatever that may mean). In your case, as I have said, you may be too exhausted to start making friends with your baby on the first day, but it is well you should know that it is entirely natural that a mother should want to get to know her baby right away after the birth. This is not only because she longs to know him, it is also—and it is this which makes it an urgent matter—because she has had all sorts of ideas of giving birth to something awful, something certainly not so perfect as a baby. It is as if human beings find it very difficult to believe that they are good enough to create within themselves something that is quite good. I doubt whether any mother really and fully believes in her child at the beginning. Father comes into this too, for he suffers just as much as mother does from the doubt that he may not be able to create a healthy normal child. Getting to know your baby is therefore in the first place an urgent matter, because of the relief the good news brings to both parents.

After this you will want to get to know your baby because of your love and pride. And then you will study him in detail so as to be able to give him the help he needs, help that he can only get from the one who knows him best, that is to say, from you, his mother.

All of this means that the care of a new-born infant is a whole-time job, and that it can be done well by only one person.

3

The Baby as a Going Concern

[1949]

I HAVE been talking generally about mothers and their own babies. I was not specially out to tell mothers what to do, because they can get advice over details quite easily from Welfare Centres. In fact advice over details comes to them almost too easily, sometimes causing a feeling of muddle. I have chosen instead to talk to those mothers who are ordinarily good at looking after their own babies, intending to help them to know what babies are like, and to show them a little of what is going on. The idea is that the more they know, the more they will be able to afford to trust their own judgment. It is when a mother trusts her own judgment that she is at her best.

It is surely tremendously important for a mother to have the experience of doing what she feels like doing, which enables her to discover the fullness of the motherliness in herself; for just as a writer is surprised by the wealth of ideas that turn up when he puts his pen to paper, so the mother is constantly surprised by what she finds in the richness of her minute to minute contact with her own baby.

In fact, one might ask how can a mother learn about being a mother in any other way than by taking full responsibility? If she just does what she is told, she has to go on doing what she is told, and to improve she can only choose somebody better to tell her what to do. But if she is feeling free to act in the way that comes naturally to her, she grows in the job.

This is where the father can help. He can help provide a space in which the mother has elbow-room. Properly protected by her man, the mother is saved from having to turn outwards to deal with her surroundings at the time when she is wanting so much to turn inwards, when she is longing to be concerned with the inside of the circle which she can make with her arms, in the centre of which is the baby. This period of time in which the mother is naturally preoccupied with the one infant does not last long. The mother's bond with the baby is very powerful at the beginning, and we must do all we can to enable her to be preoccupied with her baby at this, the natural, time.

Now it so happens that it is not only the mother that this experience is good for; the baby undoubtedly needs exactly this kind of thing too. We are only just beginning to realise how absolutely the new-born infant needs love of the mother. The health of the grown-up person is being founded throughout childhood, but the foundation of the health of the human being is laid by you in the baby's first weeks and months. Perhaps this thought can help a little when you feel strange at the temporary loss of your interest in world affairs. You are founding the health of a person who will be a member of our society. This is worth doing. The odd thing is that it is generally thought that the care of children is more difficult the greater the number being cared for. Actually I am sure that the fewer the children, the greater the emotional strain. Devotion to one child is the greatest strain of all, and it is a good job it only lasts for a while.

So here you are with all your eggs in one basket. What are you going to do about it? Well, enjoy yourself! Enjoy being thought important. Enjoy letting other people look after the world while you are producing a new one of its members. Enjoy being turned-in and almost in love with yourself, the baby is so nearly part of you. Enjoy the way in which your man feels responsible for the welfare of you and your baby. Enjoy finding out new things about yourself. Enjoy having more right than you have ever had before to do just what you feel is good. Enjoy being annoyed with the baby when cries and yells prevent acceptance of the milk that you long to be generous with. Enjoy all sorts of womanly feelings that you cannot even start to explain to a man. Particularly, I know you will enjoy the signs that gradually appear that the baby is a person, and that you are recognised as a person by the baby.

Enjoy all this for your own sake, but the pleasure which you can get out of the messy business of infant care happens to be vitally important from the baby's point of view. The baby does not want to be given the correct feed at the correct time, so much as to be fed by someone who loves feeding her own baby. The baby takes for granted all things like the softness of the clothes and having the bath water at the right temperature. What cannot be taken for granted is the mother's pleasure that goes with the clothing and bathing of her own baby. If you are there enjoying it all, it is like the sun coming out, for the baby. The mother's pleasure has to be there or else the whole procedure is dead, useless, and mechanical.

This enjoyment, which comes naturally in the ordinary way, can of course be interfered with by your worries, and worry depends a great deal on ignorance. It is rather like what you may perhaps have read about the so-called relaxation methods in childbirth. The people who write these books do all they can to explain just what happens during pregnancy and childbirth, so that mothers can relax, which means stop worrying about the unknown, and, as it were, lie back on natural processes. So much of the pain of childbirth does not belong to childbirth itself but to the tightness that comes from fear, chiefly from fear of the unknown. That is all explained to you, and if you have a good doctor and nurse available you can bear the pain which cannot be avoided.

In the same way, after the child is born, the pleasure that you get looking after the baby depends on your not being tense and worried because of ignorance and fear.

In these talks I want to give mothers information, so that they will know more than they did about what is going on in the baby, and so that they will see how the baby needs just exactly what a mother does well if she is easy, natural, and lost in the job.

I shall talk about the baby's body and what goes on inside; and I shall talk about the baby's developing person, and I shall talk about the way you introduce the world in small doses, so that the baby is not confused.

Now I want to make just one thing clear. It is this. Your baby does not depend on you for growth and development. Each baby is a *going concern*. In each baby is a vital spark, and this urge towards life and growth and development is a part of the baby, something the child is born with and which is carried forward in a way that we do not have to understand. For instance, if you have just put a bulb in the window-box you know perfectly well that you do not have to make the bulb grow into a daffodil. You supply the right kind of earth or fibre and you keep the bulb watered just the right amount, and the rest comes naturally, because the bulb has life in it. Now, the care of infants is very much more complicated than the care of a daffodil bulb, but the illustration serves my purpose because, both with the bulb and with the infant, there is something going on which is not your responsibility. The baby was conceived in you and from that moment became a lodger in your body. After birth the baby became a lodger in your arms. This is a temporary affair. It will not last for ever, in fact it will not last for long. The baby will only too soon be at school. Just at the moment this lodger is tiny and weak in body, and needing the special care that comes from your love. This does not alter the fact that the tendency towards life and growth is something inherent in the baby.

I wonder whether you feel at all relieved to hear somebody say this? I have known mothers whose enjoyment of their motherhood was spoiled by the fact that they felt somehow responsible for the aliveness of the baby. If the baby slept they would go over to the cot rather hoping that he or she would wake and so show signs of liveliness. If the baby were sullen they would play about, and poke his face, trying to produce a smile, which of course meant nothing to the infant. It was just a reaction. Such people are always jogging babies up and down on their knees trying to produce a giggle, or anything that reassures them themselves by indicating that the life process in the infant continues.

Some children are never allowed even in earliest infancy just to lie back and float. They lose a great deal, and may altogether miss the feeling that they themselves want to live. It seems to me that if I can convey to you that there really is this living process in the baby (which, as a matter of fact, it is quite difficult to extinguish) you may be better able to enjoy the care of your baby. Ultimately, life depends less on the will to live than on the fact of breathing.

Some of you have created works of art. You have done drawings and paintings, or you have moulded out of clay, or you have knitted jumpers or made dresses. When you did these things, what turned up was made by you. Babies are different. The baby grows, and you are the mother providing a suitable environment.

Some people seem to think of a child as clay in the hands of a potter. They start moulding the infant, and feeling responsible for the result. This is quite wrong. If this is what you feel, then you will be weighed down with responsibility which you need not take at all. If you can accept this idea of a baby as a going concern you are then free to get a lot of interest out of looking to see what happens in the development of the baby while you are enjoying responding to his or her needs.

4

Infant Feeding

[1944]

SINCE the beginning of this century a great deal of work has been done on infant feeding, and doctors and physiologists have written many books and innumerable scientific articles, each adding a bit to our knowledge. The result of all this work is that it is now possible to distinguish between two sets of things, those of a physical or biochemical or substantial kind, which no one could know about intuitively, or without deep learning in scientific matters, and those of a psychological kind, which people have been able to know always, both by feeling and by simple observation.

For instance, to go to the root of the matter right away, infant feeding is a matter of infant-mother relationship, a putting into practice of a love relationship between two human beings. It was difficult, however, for this to be accepted (although it was felt to be true by mothers) until many difficulties had been cleared away by study of the physical side of the problem. At any period of the world's history a natural mother leading a healthy life must easily have thought of infant feeding simply as a relationship between her baby and herself; but there was at the same time the mother whose baby died of diarrhœa and sickness; she did not know it was a germ that had killed her baby, and so she must have felt convinced that her milk was bad. Infant disease and death make mothers lose confidence in themselves, and make them look for authoritative advice. In countless ways physical disease has complicated the problem as seen by the mother. In fact, it is only because of the great advances in knowledge of physical health and physical disease that we can now return to the main thing, which is the emotional situation, the feeling bond between mother and baby. It is this feeling bond that must be developing satisfactorily if feeding is to go well.

Nowadays the doctors of the body understand enough about rickets to prevent its occurrence; they understand enough about the dangers of infection to prevent the blindness that used to follow gonococcal infection of the baby at birth; enough about the danger of tuberculous milk from infected cows to prevent much of the tuberculous meningitis that used to be common and fatal; enough about scurvy to have virtually eliminated it. And now it has suddenly become urgent for those of us who concern ourselves chiefly with feelings to state as accurately as we can the psychological problem which confronts every mother, however complete the absence of bodily disease and disorder owing to the doctors' skill.

No doubt we cannot yet accurately state the psychological problem which confronts every mother of a new-born baby, but an attempt can be made, and mothers can take part in correcting what is wrong in what I say and adding what is left out.

I will take a chance on it. If the mother we are thinking about is ordinarily healthy, living in an ordinarily tolerable home kept by her and her husband, and if we pretend that the baby arrived in a healthy state and at the right time, then there is something remarkably simple to be said: in these circumstances, infant feeding is just a part, one of the more important parts it is true, of a relationship of two human beings. These two, mother and new-born baby, are ready to be bound to each other by tremendously powerful bonds of love, and they naturally have to get to know each other before taking the great emotional risks involved. Once they have come to a mutual understanding—which they may do at once, or which they may do only after a struggle—they rely on each other and understand each other, and the feeding begins to look after itself.

In other words, if the relationship between mother and baby has started, and is developing naturally, then there is no need for feeding techniques, and weighings and all sorts of investigations; the two together know what is just right better than any outsider ever can. In such circumstances an infant will take the right amount of milk at the right speed, and will know when to stop. And in that case even the baby's digestion and excretions do not have to be watched by outsiders. The whole physical process works just because the emotional relationship is developing naturally. I would even go further and say that a mother in such circumstances can learn about babies from her baby, just as the baby learns about his mother from her.

The real trouble is that so great feelings of pleasure belong to the intimate bodily and spiritual bond that can exist between a mother and her baby that mothers easily fall a prey to the advice of people who seem to say that such feelings must not be indulged in. Surely the modern puritan is to be found in this realm of infant feeding! Fancy keeping a baby away from his mother after he is born till he has lost his one possibility (through his sense of smell) of feeling he has found her again after he had lost her! Fancy wrapping up the baby while he is feeding so that he cannot handle the breasts or the bottle, with the result that he can only take part in the proceedings by 'Yes' (sucking) or 'No' (turning the head away or sleeping)! Fancy starting off feeding a baby by the clock before he has gained the feeling that there really is anything outside himself and his desires at all.

In the natural state (by which I mean when the two human beings involved are healthy) techniques and quantities and timing can be left to nature. This means, in practice, that the mother can allow the infant to decide what it is in his power to decide, because she is easily able to decide and provide what it is her job to give in the way of management, as well as in the form of actual milk.

It may be thought imprudent of me to say these things because so few mothers are free from personal difficulties, and from that tendency to worry that makes them need support; also, there undoubtedly are mothers who neglect their babies or are cruel to them. However, it is my opinion that even mothers who know they need advice all along the line are nevertheless helped by having these basic facts in front of them. If such a mother is to learn to make a job of her second or third baby's early contact with her, she must know what she was aiming at even with her first baby over whom she needed so much help; she aims at being independent of advice in her actual management of her own babies.

I would say that natural feeding is given exactly when the baby wants it, and ceases as he ceases to want it. This is the basis. On this, and only on this, can an infant start to compromise with his mother, the first compromise being the acceptance of regular and reliable feeding, say three-hourly, which is convenient for mother, and which can yet feel to the infant like the fulfilment of his own desire, if only he can arrange to be hungry regularly at three-hourly intervals. If this interval is too long for the child in question, distress ensues, and the quickest method of restoring confidence is for the mother to feed as and when required for a new period, returning to a suitable regular timing as the baby becomes able to tolerate it.

Again, this may seem rather wild. A mother who has been schooled into training her infant to regular habits, starting with regular three-hourly feeds, feels actually wicked if told to feed her baby just like a gipsy. As I have said, she easily feels scared of the very great pleasure involved in this, and feels she will be blamed by her in-laws and the neighbours for whatever goes wrong from that day forward. The main trouble is that people easily feel overwhelmed by the responsibility of having a baby at all, and they only too readily welcome the rule and the regulation and the precept, which makes life less risky even if a trifle boring. To some extent, however, the medical and nursing professions are to blame, and we must quickly withdraw whatever we have put between the mother and her baby. Even the idea of natural feeding would be harmful if it were to become a thing to be consciously aimed at, because it was said to be good by the authorities.

As to the theory that training must start as early as possible, the truth is that training is out of place until the infant has accepted the world outside himself and come to terms with it. And the foundation of this acceptance of external reality is the first brief period in which a mother naturally follows the desires of her infant.

You see that I am not saying that we can walk out of the infant welfare centres and leave the mothers and babies to cope with all the problems of basic diet, vitamins, vaccinations, and the proper way to wash napkins. What I am saying is that doctors and nurses should be aiming at so managing this physical side that nothing can disturb the delicate mechanism of the developing infant-mother relationship.

Of course, if I were talking to nurses who look after babies who are not their own, I should have a lot to say about their difficulties and disappointments. In a remarkable book, *The Nursing Couple,*[1] my late friend Dr. Merell Middlemore wrote:

> 'It is not surprising that roughness in the nurse should some-

[1] *The Nursing Couple,* Merell P. Middlemore, M.D. Hamish Hamilton Medical Books.

> times arise from nervousness. She follows the fortunes and failures of the nursing couple from feed to feed and, up to a point, their interests are her own. She may find it hard to watch the mother's clumsy efforts to feed the child, and may at the last feel driven to interfere because she thinks she can put things right. Her own maternal instinct is, as it were, roused to compete with the mother's, instead of reinforcing it.'

Mothers reading what I have written must not be too upset if they have failed in their first contact with one of their children. There are so many reasons why there must be failures, and much can be done at a later date to make up for what has gone wrong, or has been missed. But the risk of making some mothers unhappy must be taken if one is to try to give support to those mothers who can succeed, and who are succeeding, in this the most important of all mothers' tasks. At any rate, I must risk hurting some who are in difficulties if I am to try to convey my opinion that if a mother is managing her relation to her baby *on her own,* she is doing the best that she can do for her child, for herself, and for society in general.

In other words, the only true basis for a relation of a child to mother and father, to other children, and eventually to society, is the first successful relationship between the mother and baby, between two people, with not even a regular feeding-rule coming between them, nor even a rule that baby must be breast-fed. In human affairs, the more complex can only develop out of the more simple.

5

Where the Food Goes

[1949]

When babies begin to feel hungry something is beginning to come alive in them which is ready to take possession of them. You yourself begin to make certain noises to do with the preparation of the feed which the baby knows as a sign that the time is coming when it will be safe to let eagerness for food ripen into a terrific urge. You can see saliva flowing out, because small babies don't swallow their saliva—they show the world by dribbling that they have an interest in things they can get hold of with their mouths. Well, this is only saying that the baby is getting excited, and particularly excited in the mouth. The hands also play their part in the search for satisfaction. So when you give the baby food, you are fitting in with a tremendous desire for food. The mouth is prepared. The pads on the lips are very sensitive at this time and they help to provide a high degree of pleasurable mouth sensation which the baby will never have again in later life.

A mother actively adapts to her baby's needs. She likes to. Because of her love she is expert at making delicate adjustments in her management which other people wouldn't think worth while, and wouldn't be able to know about. Whether you are feeding at the breast or the bottle, the baby's mouth becomes very active and milk goes from you or the bottle into the mouth.

There is generally thought to be a difference here between the breast- and bottle-fed baby. The breast-fed baby gets behind the root of the nipple and chews with the gums. This can be quite painful for the mother, but the pressure there pushes the milk that is in the nipple into the mouth. The milk is then swallowed. The bottle-fed baby, however, has to employ a different technique. In this case the accent is on the sucking, which can be a relatively minor matter in the breast experience.

Some babies on the bottle need a fairly large hole in the teat because they want to get the milk without sucking until they have learned to suck. Others suck right away, and get swamped if the hole is too big.

If you are using a bottle, you will have to be prepared to make changes in what you are doing in a more conscious way than you would be if you were feeding at the breast. The breast-feeding mother relaxes, she feels the blood going to her breasts, and the milk just comes. When she is bottle-feeding she has to keep her wits about her. She keeps on taking the bottle out of the baby's mouth and letting some air into it, because otherwise the vacuum in the bottle becomes so great that the baby can't get any milk out. She lets the milk cool to almost the right temperature, and tests it by putting the bottle against her arm; and she has a can of hot water by her to stand the bottle in, in case the baby is slow and the milk cools down too much.

Well, now we are concerned with what happens to the milk. We could say that the baby knows a lot about the milk up to the moment when it is swallowed. There it is going into the mouth, and giving a definite sensation to the mouth, and having a definite taste. This is undoubtedly very satisfactory. And then it is swallowed. This means it is almost lost from the baby's point of view. Fists and fingers are better in this respect, for they stay put, and remain available. Swallowed food is not completely lost, however, not while it is in the stomach. From this the food can still be returned. Babies seem to be able to know of the state of their stomachs.

You probably know that the stomach is a small organ shaped rather like a baby's bottle swung across from left to right under the ribs, and it is a muscle, rather a complicated one, with a wonderful capacity for doing just what mothers do to their babies; that is, it adapts to new conditions. It does this automatically unless disturbed by excitement, fear, or anxiety, just as mothers are naturally good mothers unless they are tense and anxious. It is rather like a miniature good mother inside. When a baby feels at ease (or what we call relaxed when we are talking about grown-up people) this muscular container, which we call the stomach, behaves itself well. That means that it keeps up a certain tension within itself and yet maintains its shape and its position.

So the milk is in the stomach, and is held there. And now starts a series of processes which we call digestion. There is always fluid in the stomach, digestive juices, and at the top end there is always air. This air has a special interest for mothers and babies. When the baby swallows the milk there is an increase in the amount of fluid in the stomach. If you and the baby are fairly calm the pressure in the stomach-wall adapts itself and loosens up a bit; the stomach gets bigger. The baby is usually a bit excited, however, and the stomach therefore takes a little while to adapt. The temporarily increased pressure in the stomach is uncomfortable, and a quick way out of the trouble is for the baby to belch a little wind. For this reason, after you have fed your baby, or even in the middle of a feed, you may find it a good idea to expect a little wind, and if the baby is upright when belching you are much more likely to get wind by itself, instead of a return of some of the milk along with it. That is why you can see mothers putting their babies up on their shoulders and just patting the back a little, because the patting stimulates the stomach muscle and makes the baby more liable to belch.

Of course it very often happens that the baby's stomach adapts so quickly to the feed, and accepts the milk so easily, that there is no need for any belching at all. But if the mother of the baby is in a tense state herself (as she may well be sometimes) then the baby gets into a tense state too, and in that case the stomach will take longer to adapt to the increase in the amount of food in it. If you understand what is going on, you will be able to manage this wind business quite easily, and you will not be puzzled when one feed is quite different from another, or when one baby is different from another baby in this matter of wind.

If you do not understand what is going on, you are bound to be flummoxed. A neighbour says to you, 'Be sure you get some wind up after the baby's feed!' Not knowing the facts you can't argue, so you plant the baby on your shoulder and vigorously pat the back, trying to get up this wind which you feel *has* to be produced. It can become a kind of religion. In that way you are imposing your own (or your neighbour's) ideas on the baby, and interfering with the natural way, which is after all the only good kind of way.

Well, this little muscular container keeps the milk for a certain length of time, until the first stage in digestion has occurred. One of the first things that happens to the milk is that it becomes curdled. That is the first stage in the natural process of digestion. In fact in making a junket you imitate what happens in the stomach. Don't be alarmed, therefore, if your baby brings up some curdled milk. It ought to be so. Also babies are very easily a little bit sick.

In this period, in which things are going on in the stomach itself, it is a very good idea if the baby is able to be quiet. Whether you manage this best by putting the baby in a cot after the feed, or by gently carrying him round for a little while, I must leave to you, because no two mothers and no two babies are alike. In the easiest circumstances the baby just lies back and seems to be contemplating the inside. There can be a good feeling inside at this time, because the blood goes to the active part, and this gives a nice warm sensation in the baby's belly. Disturbances, distractions, and excitements during this early part of the digestive processes can easily cause discontented crying, or can lead either to vomiting, or else to too early passing on of the food before it has really undergone all the changes which it should undergo in the stomach itself. I think you know how important it is to keep neighbours out when you are feeding your child. This does not apply simply to the time when you are giving the feed. The feeding time continues right on to the time when the food leaves the stomach, and it is rather like the important part of a solemn occasion which seems to be spoiled if an aeroplane passes overhead. Yes, this solemn period extends to include the period after feeding, when the food is not yet fully accepted.

If all goes well, there comes an end to this particular sensitive time, and you begin to hear gurglings and rumblings. This means that the part of the digestion of the milk which goes on in the stomach is becoming completed, and quite automatically the stomach now tends to squirt more and more of the partially digested milk through a valve into what we might call the guts.

Now, you do not have to know much about what happens in the guts. The continuation of the digestion of the milk is a very complex process, but gradually the digested milk starts to get absorbed into the blood and to be carried to every part of the body. It is interesting to know that soon after the milk leaves the stomach bile is added. This comes down from the liver at the appropriate moment, and it is because of bile that the contents of the guts have their particular colour. You may have had catarrhal jaundice yourself and so you know how horrid it feels when the bile cannot go from the liver into the guts, in that case because of inflammatory swelling in the little tube that carries it. The bile (in catarrhal jaundice) goes into your blood instead of into your guts, and makes you yellow all over. But when the bile goes the right way just at the right moment, from the liver to the guts, it makes the baby feel good.

Well, if you look it up in a physiology book you will be able to find out all that happens in the further digestion of the milk, but the details do not matter if you are a mother. The point is that the gurglings indicate that the period in which the child is sensitive is over, and the food is now really inside. From the infant's point of view this new stage must be a mystery, as physiology is beyond the infant mind. *We* know, however, that in various ways the food is absorbed from the guts, and it eventually gets distributed round the body and by means of the blood stream gets carried to every part of the tissues, which are all the time growing. In a baby these tissues are growing at a tremendous pace, and they need regularly repeated supplies.

6

The End of the Digestive Process

[1949]

IN the last talk I traced the fate of the milk as it was swallowed, digested, and absorbed. Here in the guts of the baby there is a great deal that goes on that does not concern the mother, and from the baby's point of view all this part of the process is a mystery. Gradually, however, the baby becomes involved again at the last stage, which we call excretion, and so the mother is involved too, and she can play her part best if she knows what is going on.

The fact is that the food is not all absorbed; even perfectly good breast milk leaves some kind of residue, and in any case there is the wear and tear of the guts. One way and another there is a lot left over, and it has to be got rid of.

The various things that go to make up what is going to be the motion gradually get passed on to the lower end of the guts towards the opening which is called the anus. How is this done? The stuff is moved on by a series of contraction waves which keep on going down the length of the guts. By the way, did you know that the food has to go through a narrow tube twenty feet long in a grown-up? In a baby the guts are about twelve feet long.

I sometimes have a mother say to me, 'the food went right through 'im, doctor.' It seemed to the mother that as soon as some food went into the baby it came out again at the other end. That is what it looks like, but it isn't true. The point is that the baby's guts are sensitive, and the taking of food starts up the waves of contraction in the guts; when these reach the lower end a motion is passed. Ordinarily the last part of the guts, the rectum, is more or less empty. These contraction waves get busy when there is much to be passed along, or if the baby is excited, or if the guts are inflamed by infection. Gradually, and only gradually, the infant gets some measure of control, and I want to tell you how this happens.

At first we can imagine that the rectum begins to fill simply because there is a large amount of residue waiting to pass down. Probably the actual stimulus for the bowel movement comes from the digestive process set up by the last feed. Sooner or later the rectum is filled. The infant has not known much about the stuff while it was higher up, but the filling of the rectum produces a definite sensation which is not unpleasurable, and it makes the baby want to pass the motion right out. At first we need not expect the baby to hold it in the rectum. Yon know only too well that in the early stages of infant care the changing and washing of napkins looms large. If there must be clothes, then there has to be a frequent changing of napkins, otherwise the motion left for a long time in contact with the skin causes soreness. This is especially true if for some reason or other the motion has been passed on quickly and is therefore liquid. This napkin business cannot be got rid of by hasty training. If you carry on with the good work, and play for time, then things begin to happen.

You see, if the motion is held by the baby at the last stage in the rectum, it gets dried; water is absorbed from it as it waits there. The motion is then passed on as a solid thing which the baby can enjoy passing; in fact, at the moment of passing the motion there can be such an excitement just there that the baby cries from excess of feeling. You see what you are doing by leaving the matter to your baby (although helping in so far as the baby cannot manage alone)? You are giving every possible chance for him to find from experience that it feels good to collect the stuff and hold it for a while before passing it on, and even for the baby to discover that the result is interesting, and that in fact defecation can be an extremely satisfactory experience if all goes well. The establishment of this healthy attitude of the baby towards these things is the only good foundation for anything you may want to do at a later date in the way of training.

Perhaps someone told you to hold your baby out regularly after feeds from the start, with the idea of getting in a bit of training at the earliest possible moment. If you do this you should know that what you are doing is trying to save yourself the bother of dirty napkins. And there is a lot to be said for this. But the baby is not anywhere near being able to be trained yet. If you never allow for his or her own development in these matters, you interfere with the beginnings of a natural process. Also you are missing good things. For instance, if you wait you will sooner or later discover that the baby, lying over there in the cot, finds a way of letting you know that a motion has been passed; and soon you will even get an inkling that there is going to be a motion. You are now at the beginning of a new relationship with the baby, who cannot communicate with you in an ordinary grown-up way, but who has found a way of talking without words. It is as if he said, 'I think I am going to want to pass a motion; are you interested?' and you (without exactly saying so) answer 'Yes', and you let him know that if you are interested this is not because you are frightened that he will make a mess, and not because you feel you ought to be teaching him how to be clean. If you are interested it is because you love your baby in the way mothers do, so that whatever is important to the baby is also important to you. So you will not mind if you got there late, because the important thing was not keeping the baby clean, it was the answering of the call of a fellow human being.

Later on, your relationship to the infant in these terms will become richer; sometimes a baby will feel frightened of the motion that is coming, and sometimes he will feel that it is something valuable. Because what you do is based on the simple fact of your love you soon become able to distinguish between the times when you are helping your baby to be rid of bad things, and when you are receiving gifts.

There is a practical point worth mentioning here. When a nice satisfactory motion has been passed you might think that that was the end of everything, and you pack the baby up again and get on with whatever you are doing. But the baby may show new discomfort, or may dirty the clean napkin almost immediately. It is extremely likely that a first emptying of the rectum will be followed almost immediately by a certain amount of refilling. If you are not in a hurry, and you can afford to wait, the baby will be able to pass this instalment too when the next waves of contraction come down. This might happen, and it might happen again. By not being in a hurry you leave your baby with an empty rectum. This keeps the rectum sensitive, and the next time it fills, some hours later, the baby will once more go over the whole procedure in a natural way. Mothers who are always in a hurry always have to leave their babies with something in the rectum. This will either be passed out, causing unnecessary dirtying of napkins, or else it will be held in the rectum which therefore becomes less sensitive, and the beginnings of the next experience will be interfered with to some extent. Unhurried management over a long period of time naturally lays the basis for a sense of order in the baby's relation to his excretory functions. If you are in a hurry, and cannot allow for the total experience, the baby will start off in a muddle. The baby who is not in a muddle will be able to follow you later on, and gradually give up some of the tremendous pleasure that belongs to the doing of a motion just exactly when the impulse comes. The baby does this not simply to comply with your wish that as few messes as possible be made, but out of a wish to wait for you, so as to get into touch with your liking to look after all that has to do with your own baby. Much later on the baby will be able to gain control down there, and to make messes, when the idea is to dominate over you, and to hold things back till the convenient moment comes, when the idea is to please you.

I could tell you about plenty of babies who never had a chance to find themselves in this important matter of the passing of motions. I know of a mother who practically never let any of her babies have a natural motion. She had a theory that the motion in the rectum poisons the baby in some way or other. This is simply not true; and babies and small children can hold their motions there for days without being really harmed. This mother was always interfering with each baby's rectum with soapsticks and enemas, and the result was more than chaotic. Certainly she had no hope whatever of producing happy children who could easily be fond of her.

You will, no doubt, expect me also to talk about the other kind of excretion, the passing of urine. The general principles are the same in both.

Water is absorbed into the blood stream, and what is not needed is excreted by the baby's kidneys and passed to the bladder along with waste products dissolved in it. The baby does not know anything till the bladder begins to fill, and then there develops an urge to pass the urine out. At first this is more or less automatic, but the baby gradually finds that there is a reward for holding back a little —after holding back the baby finds it pleasurable to get rid of the water. There develops another little orgy that enriches the life of the infant, that makes life worth living, and the body worth living in.

In the course of time this discovery of the infant, that waiting pays, can be used by you, because you can get to know by signs that something may be going to happen, and you can still further enrich the baby's experience by your interest in the procedure. In time the baby will like to wait, if not too long, just in order to get the whole thing within the love relationship that exists between the two of you.

You see how it is that the baby's mother is needed for the management of the excretions, just as she is needed for the feeding? Only the mother feels it is worth while to follow the infant's needs in detail, so enabling the exciting experiences of the body to become part of a love relationship between two persons, the baby and herself.

When this is what happens, and when it is kept up over a period of time, what is called training can follow without much difficulty, because the mother has earned the right to make such demands as are not beyond the infant's capacity.

Here again is an example of the way in which the foundations of health are laid down by the ordinary mother in her ordinary loving care of her own baby.

7

The Baby as a Person

[1949]

I HAVE been wondering how to start to describe babies as persons. It is easy to see that when food goes into the baby it is digested, and some of it is distributed round the body and used for growth. Some of it is stored as energy, and some of it is got rid of in one way or another. That is looking at the baby with an interest in bodies. But if we look at the same baby, being interested in the person that is there, we can easily see that there is an imaginative feeding experience, as well as this bodily one. The one is based on the other.

I think you can get quite a lot out of thinking that all the things that you do because of your love of the baby go in just like the food. The baby builds something out of it all, and not only that, but the baby has phases of making use of you and then dropping you, just in the same way as with the food. Perhaps I can explain what I mean best by letting him suddenly grow up a little.

Here is a ten-month-old baby boy. He is sitting on his mother's knee while the mother is talking to me. He is lively and awake, and naturally interested in things. Instead of just letting everything get into a muddle I place an attractive object on the corner of the table, between where I am sitting and where the mother is sitting. The mother and I can go on talking, but out of the corner of one eye we can watch the baby. You may be sure that if he is just an ordinary baby he will notice the attractive object (let us call it a spoon), and he will reach for it. As a matter of fact, probably as soon as he has reached for it, he will suddenly be overcome with reserve. It is as if he thought, 'I had better think this thing out:

I wonder what feelings mother will have on this subject. I had better hold back until I know'. So he will turn away from the spoon as if nothing were further from his thoughts. In a few moments, however, he will return to his interest in it, and he will very tentatively put a finger on the spoon. He may perhaps grasp it, and look at mother to see what he can get from her eyes. At this point I will probably have to tell mother what to do, because otherwise she will help too much, or hinder as the case may be; so I ask her to play as small a part in what happens as possible.

Well, he gradually finds from his mother's eyes that this new thing he is doing is not disapproved of, and so he catches hold of the spoon more firmly and begins to make it his own. He is still very tense, however, because he is not certain what will happen if he does with this thing what he wants to do so badly. He does not even know for sure what it is that he wants to do.

We guess that in the course of a little while he will discover what he wants to do with it, because his mouth begins to get excited. He is still very quiet and thoughtful, but saliva begins to flow from his mouth. His tongue looks sloppy. His mouth begins to want the spoon. His gums begin to want to enjoy biting on it. It is not very long before he has put it in his mouth. Then he has feelings about it in the ordinary aggressive way that belongs to lions and tigers, and babies, when they get hold of something good. He makes as if to eat it.

We can now say that the baby has taken this thing and made it his own. He has lost all the stillness that belongs to concentration, and wondering, and doubt. Instead he is confident, and very much enriched by the new acquisition. I would say that in imagination he has eaten it. Just as the food goes in and is digested and becomes part of him, so this which has been made his own in an imaginative way is now part of himself and can be used. How will it be used?

Well, you know the answer because this is only a special case of what is going on all the time at home. He will put it to mother's mouth to feed her, and he will want her to play at eating it. Mind you, he does not want her to bite it really, and he would be rather frightened if she actually let it go into her mouth. It's a game; it is an exercise of the imagination. He is playing, and he invites play. What else will he do? He will feed me, and he may want me to play at eating it too. He may make a gesture towards the mouth of someone on the other side of the room. Let everybody share this good thing. He has had it; why shouldn't every one have it? He has something he can be generous with. Now he puts it inside his mother's blouse where her breast is, and then rediscovers it and takes it out again. Now he shoves it under the blotting pad and enjoys the game of losing it and finding it again, or he notices a bowl on the table and starts scooping imaginary food out of the bowl, imaginatively eating his broth. The experience is a rich one. It corresponds to the mystery of the middle of the body, the digestive processes, the time between when the food is lost by being swallowed, and when the residue is rediscovered at the lower end in the fæces and urine. I could go on for a long time describing how different babies show that they are enriched by this kind of playing.

Now the baby has dropped the spoon. I suppose his interest began to get transferred on to something else. I will pick it up and he can take it again. Yes, he seems to want it, and he takes up the game again, using the spoon as before, as an extra bit of himself. Oh, he's dropped it again! Evidently it was not quite by chance that he dropped it. Perhaps he likes the sound of the spoon as it falls on the floor. We will see. I will hand it to him again. Now he just takes it and drops it quite deliberately; dropping it is what he wants to do. Once again I give it back to him, and he practically throws it away. He is now reaching out for other interests, the spoon is finished with; we have come to the end of the show.

We have watched the baby develop an interest in something, and make it part of himself, and we have watched him use it, and then finish with it. This sort of thing is going on all the time at home, but the sequence is more obvious in this special setting, which gives time for the baby to go right through an experience.

What have we learned watching this little baby boy?

For one thing, we have witnessed a completed experience. Because of the controlled circumstances there could be a beginning, a middle, and an end to what happened; there was a total happening. *This is good for the baby.* When you are in a hurry, or are harassed, you cannot allow for *total happenings,* and your baby is the poorer. When you have time, however, as you certainly should have when you have care of a baby, you can allow for these. Total happenings enable babies to catch hold of time. They do not start off knowing that when something is on it will finish.

Do you see how the middle of things can be enjoyed (or if bad, tolerated) only if there is a strong sense of start and finish?

By allowing your baby time for total experiences, and by taking part in them, you gradually lay a foundation for the child's ability eventually to enjoy all sorts of experiences without jumpiness.

Another thing we can get out of watching that baby with the spoon. We saw how there came doubt and hesitation at the start of a new venture. We watched the child stretch out and touch and handle the spoon, and after the first simple reaction he temporarily withdrew interest. Then, by carefully sensing the feelings of his mother, he allowed interest to return. He was tense and uncertain, however, till he had actually got the spoon to his mouth and had chewed it.

At first your baby is ready to consult you, if you are there when new situations arise. So you will need to know clearly what to let the baby touch, and what not to allow. The simplest way is the best, and this is to avoid having things around that the baby must not take and mouth. You see, the baby is trying to get at the principles that underlie your decisions, so as eventually to be able to foretell what you allow. A little later words will help, and you will say 'too sharp', 'too hot', or in some other way indicate danger to the body; or you will have a way of letting it be known that your engagement ring, put on one side while you are washing, is not put there for the baby's benefit.

Do you see how you can help your baby to avoid being in a muddle about what is good and what is bad to touch? You do this simply by being clear yourself as to what you prohibit, and why; and by being there on the spot, a preventer rather than a curer. Also, you deliberately provide things that the baby will like to handle and chew.

Another thing. We could talk of what we saw in terms of skills, the baby learning to reach out and to find and to grasp, and to put an object to the mouth. I am surprised when a baby of six months goes through this whole performance. On the other hand the interests of a child of fourteen months are too varied for us to expect to see anything so clearly as we saw with our ten-month-old baby boy.

But I think the best thing we learned watching the baby was

this. *We saw by what happened that he is not just a body, he is a person.*

The ages at which various kinds of skill develop are interesting to record, but there was more in this than skill. There was play. By playing, the baby showed that he had built up something in himself that could be called material for play, an inner world of imaginative liveliness, which the playing expresses.

Who can say how early there are the beginnings of this imaginative life of the infant, which enriches and is enriched by the bodily experience? At three months a baby may want to put a finger in mother's mouth, playing at feeding her, while taking milk at the breast. And what about the earlier weeks? Who knows? A tiny baby may want to suck a fist or finger, while taking from breast or bottle (having cake *and* eating it, so to speak), and this shows that there is something more than just a need for the satisfaction of hunger.

But to whom am I talking? Mothers have no difficulty in seeing the person in their own babies from the start. But there are people who tell you that until they are six months old babies are nothing but bodies and reflexes. Don't be put off by people who talk like that, will you?

Enjoy finding what there is to be found, as it turns up, of the person your baby is, because the baby needs this of you. So you will be ready waiting, without hurry, fuss, or impatience, for the baby's playfulness. It is this, above all, which indicates the existence of a personal inner life in the baby. If it meets in yourself a corresponding playfulness the inner richness of the baby blossoms out, and your playing together becomes the best part of the relationship between the two of you.

8

Close-up of Mother Feeding Baby

[1949]

I HAVE said, in a previous talk, that the baby appreciates, perhaps from the very beginning, the *aliveness* of the mother. The pleasure the mother takes in what she does for the infant very quickly lets the infant know that there is a human being behind what is done. But what eventually makes the baby feel the person in the mother is perhaps the mother's special ability to put herself in the place of the infant, and so to know what the infant is feeling like. No book rules can take the place of this feeling a mother has for her infant's needs, which enables her to make at times an almost exact adaptation to those needs.

I will illustrate this by looking at the feeding situation, and by comparing two babies. One of them is fed by the mother at home, and the other is fed in an institution, a nice place, but a place where the nurses have a lot to do and there is no time for individual attention.

I will take the baby in the institution first. Hospital nurses who read this, and who do feed the babies in their care individually, must forgive me for using as an illustration the worst, and not the best, of what they can do.

Here then is the baby in the institution at feed-time, hardly knowing yet what to expect. The baby that we are considering does not know much about bottles or about people, but is beginning to be prepared to believe that something satisfactory may turn up. The baby is propped up a little in the cot, and a bottle with milk is so arranged with pillows that it reaches his mouth. The nurse puts the teat into the baby's mouth, waits for a few moments, and then goes off to look after some other baby who is crying. At first things may go fairly well, because the hungry baby is stimulated to suck from the teat and the milk comes, and it feels nice; but there the thing is, sticking in the mouth, and in a few moments it has become a sort of huge threat to existence. The baby cries or struggles, then the bottle drops out, and this produces relief, but only for a little while, because soon the baby begins to want to have another go, and the bottle does not come, and then crying restarts. After a while the nurse comes back and puts the bottle in the baby's mouth again, but by now the bottle, which looks the same as it did, from our point of view, seems to the baby like a bad thing. It has become dangerous. This goes on and on.

Now let us go over to the other extreme, to the baby whose own mother is available. When I see in what a delicate way a mother who is not anxious manages the same situation I am always astounded. You see her there, making the baby comfortable, and arranging a *setting* in which the feeding may happen, if all goes well. The setting is a part of a human relationship. If the mother is feeding by the breast we see how she lets the baby, even a tiny one, have the hands free so that as she exposes her breast the texture of the skin can be felt, and its warmth—moreover the distance of her breast from the baby can be measured, for the baby has only a little bit of the world in which to place objects, the bit that can be reached by mouth, hands, and eyes. The mother allows the baby's face to touch the breast. At the beginning babies do not know about breasts being part of mother. If the face touches the breast they do not know at the beginning whether the nice feeling comes in the breast or in the face. In fact babies play with their cheeks, and scratch them, just as if they were breasts, and there is plenty of reason why mothers allow for all the contact that a baby wants. No doubt a baby's sensations in these respects are very acute, and if they are acute we can be sure they are important.

The baby first of all needs all these rather *quiet* experiences which I am describing, and needs to feel held lovingly, that is, in an alive way, yet without fuss, and anxiety, and tenseness. This is the setting. Sooner or later there will be some kind of contact between the mother's nipple and the baby's mouth. It does not matter what exactly happens. The mother is there in the situation and part of it, and she particularly likes the intimacy of the relationship. She comes without preconceived notions as to how the baby ought to behave.

This contact of the nipple with the baby's mouth gives the baby ideas!—'perhaps there is something there outside the mouth worth going for'. Saliva begins to flow; in fact, so much saliva may flow that the baby may enjoy swallowing it, and for a time hardly needs milk. Gradually the mother enables the baby to build up in imagination the very thing that she has to offer, and the baby begins to mouth the nipple, and to get to the root of it with the gums and bite it, and perhaps to suck.

And then there is a pause. The gums let go of the nipple, and the baby turns away from the scene of action. The idea of the breast fades.

Do you see how important this last bit is? The baby had an idea, and the breast with the nipple came, and a contact was made. Then the baby was finished with the idea and turned away, and the nipple disappeared. This is one of the most important ways in which the experience of the baby we are now describing differs from that of the one that we placed in the busy institution. How does the mother deal with the baby's turning away? This baby does not have a thing pushed back into the mouth in order that sucking movements shall be started up again. The mother understands what the baby is feeling, because she is alive and has an imagination. She waits. In the course of a few minutes, or less, the baby turns once more towards where she is all the time willing to place the nipple, and so a new contact is made, just at the right moment. These conditions are repeated time and again, and the baby drinks not from a thing that contains milk, but from a personal possession lent for the moment to a person who knows what to do with it.

The fact that the mother is able to make such delicate adaptation shows that she is a human being, and the baby is not long in appreciating this fact.

I want to make rather a special thing out of the way the mother in our second illustration lets the baby turn away. It is especially here, where she takes the nipple away from the baby as the baby ceases to want it or to believe in it, that she establishes herself as the mother. This is such a delicate operation at the beginning that the mother cannot always succeed, and sometimes a baby will show a need to establish the right to the personal way by refusing food, turning the head away, or going to sleep. This is very disappointing for a mother who is longing to get on with being generous. Sometimes she cannot stand the tension in the breasts (unless someone has told her how to express milk so that she can afford to wait till the baby turns towards her). If mothers knew, however, that the turning away of the baby from the breast or from the bottle had a value, they might be able to manage these difficult phases. They would take the turning away, or the sleepiness, as an indication for special care. This means that everything must be done in the way of providing the right setting for the feed. The mother must be comfortable. The baby must be comfortable. Then there must be time to spare. And the baby's arms must be free. The baby must be able to have skin free with which to feel the skin of the mother. It may even be that a baby needs to be put naked on the mother's naked body. If there is difficulty, the one thing that is absolutely no use at all is the attempt to force the feeding. If there is a difficulty, it is only by giving the baby the setting to find the breast that there is any hope of establishing the right kind of feeding experience. Echoes of all this may appear at later stages in the infant's experiences.

While I am on this subject, I would like to talk about the position of the mother whose baby is just born. She has been through an anxious and severe experience, and she continues to need skilled help. She is still in the care of whoever has helped with the confinement. There are reasons why she is particularly liable just at this time to feel dependent, and to be sensitive to the opinions of any important woman who happens to be around, whether this be the matron of the hospital, or the midwife, or her own mother or mother-in-law. She is in a difficult position then. She has been preparing for this moment for nine months, and for reasons that I have tried to explain she is the best person to know what to do to get her baby to feed at the breast, and yet if the others who know so much are strong-minded, she can hardly be expected to fight them, certainly not until she has had two or three babies, and a lot of experience. The ideal thing, of course, is the happy relationship that often exists between maternity nurses or the midwife, and the mother.

If there is this happy relationship, the mother is given every chance to manage the first contact with the baby in her own way. The baby is beside her asleep most of the time, and she can keep on looking down into the cradle beside the bed to see whether it really is a nice human baby she has got. She gets used to her own baby's cry. If she is worried by the crying the baby is temporarily taken away while she sleeps, but is brought back. Then, when she senses that the baby begins to want food, or perhaps to want a general contact with her body, she is helped to take the baby into her arms and to nurse him. In the course of this sort of experience there starts the special contact between the baby's face, mouth, and hands, and her breasts.

One hears of the young mother who is bewildered. Nothing is explained to her; the baby is kept away in another room, perhaps along with other babies, except at feed-times. There is always a baby crying, so that the mother never gets to know the cry of her own baby. At feed-times the babies are brought in and handed to their mothers, wrapped round tightly with a towel. The mother is supposed to take this queer-looking object and breast-feed it (I say 'it' on purpose), but neither does she feel the life welling up in her breasts, nor does the baby have a chance to explore, and to have ideas. One even hears of so-called helpers who get exasperated when the baby does not start sucking, and who push the baby's nose in it, so to speak. There will be a few who have had this sort of horrid experience.

But even mothers have to learn how to be motherly by experience. I think it is much better if they look at it in that way. By experience they grow. If they look at it the other way and think that they must work hard at books to learn how to be perfect mothers from the beginning, they will be on the wrong tack. In the long run, what we need is mothers, as well as fathers, who have found out how to believe in themselves. These mothers and their husbands build the best homes in which babies can grow and develop.

9

Why do Babies Cry?

[1944]

We have considered some very obvious things about your wish to know your baby and your baby's need to be known. Just as babies need mother's milk and warmth, so do they need her love and understanding. If you know your baby you are in a position to give the help he wants just when he wants it, and as no one can know a baby as well as his mother can—no one but you can be the right person to help him. Let us now consider the times when he seems to be especially asking for help—when he cries.

As you know, most babies cry a lot, and you are constantly having to decide whether to let your baby go on crying or to soothe him, or feed him, or to tell father to have a go, or to hand him over lock, stock, and barrel to the woman upstairs who knows all about children, or thinks she does. You probably wish that I could tell you quite simply what to do, but if I did you would say, 'What a fool! There are all sorts of different reasons why babies cry, and you cannot say what to do until you have found out what the crying is about.' Exactly so, and for this reason I am going to try to sort out with you the reasons for crying.

Let us say that there are four kinds of crying, because that is more or less true, and we can hang all that we want to say on these four pegs: Satisfaction, Pain, Rage, Grief. You will be able to see that really I am saying quite ordinary obvious things, the sort of thing that every mother of an infant knows naturally though she has not usually tried thinking out how to express what she knows in words.

What I am saying is no more than this, that crying is either giving the baby the feeling that he is exercising his lungs (satisfaction), or else it is a signal of distress (pain), or else it is an expression of anger (rage), or else it is a song of sadness (grief). If you will accept this as a working proposition I can explain just what I mean.

You may think it strange that I should be talking first about crying for satisfaction, almost for pleasure, because any one would admit that whenever a baby is crying he must be to some extent in distress. Yet I do think that this is really the first thing to be said. We have to recognise that pleasure enters into crying as it does into the exercise of any bodily function, so that a certain amount of crying can sometimes be said to be satisfactory for the infant, whereas less than that amount would not have been enough.

A mother will tell me, 'My baby seldom cries, except just before feeding. Of course he cries for an hour between four and five every day, but I think he likes it. He is not really in trouble, and I let him see I am about but do not especially try to soothe him.'

Sometimes you may hear people saying that a baby ought never to be picked up when he cries. We will deal with them later. But some other people say that a baby should never be allowed to cry. I feel that these people probably tell mothers not to let babies put their fists into their mouths, or suck their thumbs, or use a dummy, or play about at the breast after serious feeding is over. They do not know that babies have (and have to have) their own ways of dealing with their own troubles.

Anyway, babies who seldom cry are not necessarily, because of their not crying, doing better than babies who cry like billy-o, and, personally, if I had to choose between the two extremes, I would bet on the crying baby, who had come to know the full extent of his capacity to make a noise, provided the crying had not been allowed too often to go over into despair.

What I am saying now is that any exercise of the body is good, from the infant's point of view. Breathing itself, a new achievement to the new-born, may be quite interesting until it is taken for granted, and screaming and yelling and all forms of crying must be definitely exciting. The importance of our recognising this, the value of crying, is that we can then see how crying works as a reassurance in time of trouble. Babies cry because they feel anxious or insecure, and it works; the crying helps a lot, and we must therefore agree that there is something good about it. Later comes talking, and in time the toddler will be banging on a drum.

You know how your infant uses his fist or his finger, how he pushes it into his mouth and so manages to stand frustration. Well, screaming is like a fist that comes up from inside. And no one can interfere. You can hold your baby's hands away from his mouth, but you cannot pin his crying down into his stomach. You cannot altogether stop your baby from crying and I hope you will not try. If you have neighbours who cannot stand the noise, you are unlucky, because then you have to take steps to stop the crying on account of *their* feelings, which is a different thing from studying the reasons why your baby cries, so as to be able to prevent or stop only the crying that is unhelpful and possibly harmful.

Doctors say that the lusty cry of the new-born infant is a sign of health and strength. Well, crying goes on being a sign of health and strength, an early form of P.T., an exercise of a function, satisfying as such, and even pleasurable. *But it is very much more than this,* so now what about the other meanings of crying?

No one will find it in the least difficult to recognise the cry of pain, nature's way of letting you know your baby is in trouble and needs your help.

When a baby is in pain he utters a shrill or piercing sound, and often at the same time gives some indication of where the trouble lies. For instance, if he has colic, he draws up his legs; if it is earache, he puts a hand up towards the bad ear; if it is a bright light that is worrying him he may turn his head away. He does not know what to do about loud bangs.

The cry of pain is not in itself pleasurable to the infant and no one would think it was, because it immediately awakes in the people around the urge to do something about it.

One kind of pain is called hunger. Yes, I think hunger does seem like a pain to the infant. Hunger hurts him in a way that is apt to be forgotten by grown-ups, who quite seldom get hungry painfully. In the British Isles to-day I suppose very few know what it is to be painfully hungry. Think of all that we do to ensure a supply of food, even in wartime. We wonder what we shall eat, but we seldom wonder whether we shall eat. And if we are short of something we like, we go off it and stop wanting it, rather than go on wanting it and not getting it. But our infants know only too well the pains and pangs of acute hunger. Mothers like their infants to be nice and greedy, to get excited as they hear the noise, and see the sights, and smell the smells that advertise the fact that food is due; and excited babies are feeling pain and show it by crying. This pain is soon forgotten if it leads to satisfactory feeding.

The cry of pain is something that we hear any time after the baby's birth. Sooner or later we notice a new kind of painful crying, the crying of apprehension. I think that this means that the baby is getting to know a thing or two. He has come to know that in certain circumstances he must *expect* pain. As you start to undress him he knows he is to be taken out of comfortable warmth, he knows his position will be changed this way and that, and that all feeling of security will be lost, and so he cries as you undo his top button. He has put two and two together, he has had experiences, and one thing reminds him of another. Naturally all this becomes more and more complex as the weeks go by, and as he gets older.

As you know, a baby sometimes cries when he is dirty. This might mean that the baby does not like being dirty (and, of course, if he remains dirty long enough his skin will become chafed and hurt him), but usually it means nothing of the kind—it means that he fears the disturbance he has learned to expect. Experience has shown him that the next few minutes will bring about a failure of all the reassurances, that is to say he will be uncovered, and moved, and he will lose heat.

The basis of the crying of fear is pain, and that is why the crying sounds the same in each case, but it is pain remembered and expected to recur. After a baby has experienced any painfully acute feelings he may cry from fear when anything happens which threatens to make him have those feelings again. And quite soon he begins to develop ideas, some of them frightening, and here again, if he cries, the trouble is that something is reminding the baby of pain, although that something is imaginary.

If you have only just started thinking about these things, it may seem to you that I am making it all rather difficult and complicated, but I cannot help it and, fortunately, the next bit is as easy as winking, for the third cause of crying on my list is rage.

We all know what it is like to lose our tempers and we all know how anger, when it is very intense, sometimes seems to possess us so that we cannot for the time being control ourselves. Your baby knows about being all-out angry. However much you try, you will disappoint him at times, and he will cry in anger; according to my view you have one consolation—that angry crying probably means that he has some belief in you. He hopes he may change you. A baby who has lost belief does not get angry, he just stops wanting, or else he cries in a miserable, disillusioned way, or else he starts banging with his head on the pillow, or on the wall or the floor, or else he exploits the various things he can do with his body.

It is a healthy thing for a baby to get to know the full extent of his rage. You see, he certainly will not *feel* harmless when he is angry. You know what he looks like. He screams and kicks and, if he is old enough, he stands up and shakes the bars of the cot. He bites and scratches, and he may spit and spew and make a mess. If he really is determined he can hold his breath and go blue in the face, and even have a fit. For a few minutes he really intends to destroy or at least to spoil every one and everything, and he does not even mind if he destroys himself in the process. Don't you see that every time a baby goes through this process he gains something? If a baby cries in a state of rage and feels as if he has destroyed every one and everything, and yet the people round him remain calm and unhurt, this experience greatly strengthens his ability to see that what he feels to be true is not necessarily real, that fantasy and fact, both important, are nevertheless different from each other. There is absolutely no need for you to try to make him angry, for the simple reason that there are plenty of ways in which you cannot help making him angry whether you like it or not.

Some people go about the world terrified of losing their tempers, afraid of what would have happened if they had experienced rage to the fullest extent when they were infants. For some reason or other this never got properly tested out. Perhaps their mothers were scared. By calm behaviour they might have given confidence, but they muddled things up by acting as if the angry baby was really dangerous.

A baby in a rage is very much a person. He knows what he wants, he knows how he might get it, and he refuses to give up hope. At first he hardly knows that he has weapons. At first he can scarcely know that his yells hurt, any more than he knows that his messes give trouble. But in the course of a few months he begins to feel dangerous and to feel he can hurt and to feel he wants to hurt; and sooner or later, from personal experience of pain, he gets to know that others can suffer pain and get tired.

You can get much interest out of watching your infant for the first signs that he knows he can hurt you, and that he intends to hurt you.

Now I want to get down to the fourth on the list of the causes of crying—grief. I know that I do not have to describe sadness to you, any more than I should have to describe colour to someone not suffering from colour blindness. Yet it is not good enough for me just to mention sadness and leave it at that, for various reasons. One is that the feelings of infants are very direct and intense, and we grown-ups, although we value these intense feelings of our infancy, and like to recapture them at chosen times, have learned long since how to defend ourselves from being at the mercy of almost unbearable feelings, such as we were liable to as babies. If by the loss of someone we love deeply we cannot avoid painful grief, we just settle down to a period of mourning, which our friends understand and tolerate. And from this we may be expected sooner or later to recover. We do not just lay ourselves open to acute grief at any moment of the day or night as babies do. In fact many people defend themselves against painful grief so well that they cannot take things as seriously as they would like to take them; they cannot feel the deep feelings which they would like to feel, because they are afraid of anything so real. And they find themselves unable to take the risks involved in loving a definite person or thing; spreading their risks they may lose a lot, though they gain through being well insured against grief. How people love a sad film that makes them shed tears, which shows at least that they have not lost the art! When I talk about grief as a cause of infant crying I have to remind you that you will not easily remember the grief that belongs to your own infancy, and that therefore you will not be able to believe in your own infant's grief by direct sympathy.

Even babies can develop powerful defences against painful sadness. But I am trying to describe to you the sad crying of infants which does exist, and which you have almost certainly heard. I should like to be able to help you to see the place of sad crying and its meaning and value, so that you may know what to do when you hear it.

I am suggesting to you that when your infant shows that he can cry from sadness you can infer that he has travelled a long way in the development of his feelings; and yet I am saying, as I said about rage, that you would gain nothing by *trying to cause* sad crying. You will not be able to help making him sad any more than you can help making him angry. But there is a difference here between rage and grief, because whereas rage is a more or less direct reaction to frustration, grief implies quite complex goings-on in the infant's mind, which I will try to describe.

But first a word about the sound of sad crying, which I think you will agree has a musical note in it. Some people think that sad crying is one of the main roots of the more valuable kind of music. And by sad crying an infant to some extent entertains himself. He may easily develop and experiment with the various tones of his crying while he is waiting for sleep to come to drown his sorrows. A little older, and he will be actually heard sadly singing himself to sleep. Also, as you know, tears belong more to sad crying than to rage, and inability to cry sadly means dry eyes and a dry nose (into which the tears flow when they do not dribble down the face). So tears are healthy, both physically and psychologically.

Perhaps I could give an illustration to explain to you what I mean about the value of sadness. I will take an eighteen-month-old child because it is easier to believe in what happens at this age than in the same things happening more obscurely in earlier infancy. This little girl had been adopted at four months and had had unfortunate experiences before adoption, and for this reason was specially dependent on her mother. One could say that she had not been able to build up in her mind, as well as more fortunate babies are able to do, the idea that there are good mothers about; and for this reason she clung to the actual person of her adoptive mother, who was excellent in her care of her. The child's need of the actual presence of her adoptive mother was so great that the mother knew she must not leave the child. When the infant was seven months old she had once left her in excellent hands for half a day, but the result was nearly disastrous. Now, when the child was eighteen months old, the mother decided to take a fortnight's holiday, telling the child all about it, and leaving her in the hands of people she knew well. The child spent most of the fortnight trying the handle of her mother's bedroom door, too anxious to play, and not really accepting the fact of her mother's absence. She was much too frightened to be sad. I suppose one would say that, for her, the world stood still for a fortnight. When at last the mother came back, the child waited a little while to make sure that what she saw was real, and then she flung her arms around her mother's neck and lost herself in sobbing and deep sadness, after which she returned to her normal state.

You see how the sadness was there before the mother came back, looking at it from our point of view as outsiders. But from the little girl's point of view there was no sadness until she knew she could be sad with her mother there, her tears dropping down on to her mother's neck. Why should this be so? Well, I think we may have to say that this little girl had to cope with something which frightened her very much, that is to say with the hate of her mother that she felt when her mother left her. I chose this illustration because the fact that the child was dependent on her actual mother (and could not easily find motherliness in other people) makes it easy for us to see how dangerous the child would feel it to be to hate her mother. So she waited till her mother came back.

But what did she do when the mother came back? She might have gone up to her and bitten her. I should not be at all surprised if some of you have had such an experience. But this child flung her arms round her mother's neck and sobbed. What was mother to understand by this? If she had put it into words, which I am glad to say she did not, she would have said, 'I am your only good mother. You were frightened to find you hated me for going away. You are sorry you hated me. Not only that, you felt that I went away because of something bad you had done, or because you made such great demands on me, or because you hated me before I went; so you felt that you were the cause of my going away—you felt I was gone for ever. It was not till I was back and you had your arms round my neck that you could acknowledge that you had it in you to send me away, even while I was with you. By your sadness you earned the right to put your arms round my neck, because you showed that you felt that when I hurt you by going away it was your fault. In fact, you felt guilty, as if you were the cause of everything bad in the world, whereas really you were only a little bit the cause of my going away. Babies are a trouble, but mothers expect them to be and like them to be. Through being extra dependent on me you have been extra liable to tire me out; but I chose to adopt you, and I never feel resentment at being tired out by you . . .'

Yes, she might have said all this, but thank goodness she did not, and as a matter of fact these ideas never entered her mind. She was much too busy cuddling her little girl.

Why have I said all these things about a little girl's sobbing? I am sure no two people would describe what is going on when a child is sad in the same way, and I dare say that some of what I said is not quite rightly put. But it is not all wrong, and I am hoping that by what I have said I have been able to show you that sad crying is something very complicated, something which means that your infant has already gained his place in the world. He is no longer a cork floating on the waves. He has already started to take responsibility for environment. Instead of just reacting to circumstances he has come to feel responsible for the circumstances. The trouble is that he starts off feeling *totally* responsible for what happens to him and for the external factors in his life. Only gradually does he sort out what he *is* responsible for from all that he *feels* responsible for.

Now let us compare sad crying with the other kinds. You can see that crying from pain and hunger can be noted any time from birth onwards. Rage appears as the infant becomes able to put two and two together, and fear, indicating pain expected, means that the baby has developed ideas. Grief indicates something far in advance of these other acute feelings; and if mothers understand how valuable the things are underlying sadness they will be able to avoid missing something important. People easily find themselves glad later on when their child says 'Thank you' and 'I am sorry', but the earlier version of this is contained in the infant's sad crying, and this is much more valuable than what is taught in the way of the expression of gratitude and repentance.

You will have noted in my description of the sad little girl how it was perfectly logical for her to be sad on her mother's neck. An angry baby would scarcely be expected to be angry while in a satisfactory relation to mother. If he stayed on her lap it would be because he was afraid to leave it, and mother would probably wish he would go away. But the sad baby can be taken and cuddled because, by his taking responsibility for what hurts him, he earns the right to keep a good relation to people. In fact a sad baby may *need* your physical and demonstrative love. What he does not need, however, is to be jogged and tickled, and in other ways distracted from his sadness. Let us say he is in a state of mourning and requires a certain length of time to recover from it. He just needs to know that you continue to love him, and it may even be best sometimes to let him lie crying on his own. Remember that there is no better feeling in infancy or childhood than that which belongs to true spontaneous recovery from sadness and guilt feelings. This is so true that sometimes you will find your child being naughty so as to feel guilty and cry, and then feel forgiven, so eager is he to recapture what he has experienced as true recovery from sadness.

So now I have described various kinds of crying. There is so very much more to be said. But I think you may have been helped by my attempt to sort out one kind from another. What I have not done is to describe the crying of hopelessness and despair, the crying that the other kinds break down into if there is no hope left in the baby's mind. In your home you may never hear this kind of crying, and if you do the situation has got beyond you, and you are in need of help, although, as I have tried to make especially clear, you are otherwise much better than any one else can be in the management of your own infant. It is in institutions that we hear the crying of helplessness and disintegration, where there is no means of providing one mother for each baby. I only mention this kind of crying for the sake of completeness. For the fact that you are willing to devote yourself to the care of your infant means that he is lucky; unless something should happen by chance to upset your routine management, he will be able to go straight ahead, letting you know when he is angry with you and when he loves you, and when he wants to be rid of you, and when he is anxious or frightened, and when he just wants you to understand that he feels sadness.

10

The World in Small Doses

[1949]

If you listen to philosophical discussions you sometimes hear people using a lot of words over the business of what is real and what is not real. One person says that real means what we can all touch, see, and hear, while another says it is only what feels real that counts, like a nightmare, or hating the man who jumps the bus queue. This sounds all very difficult. Why in the world, then, should I drag these things into a talk to mothers about the management of babies? I hope I will be able to explain.

Mothers with babies are dealing with a developing, changing situation; the baby starts off not knowing about the world, and by the time they have finished their job the baby is grown up into someone who knows about the world and can find a way to live in it, and even to take part in the way it behaves. What a tremendous development!

But you will know people who have difficulties in their relation to the things that we call real. They do not feel them to be real. For you and me things feel more real sometimes than at other times. Any one may have a dream that feels more real than reality, and for some people their personal imaginative world is so much more real to them than what we call the real world that they cannot make a good job of living in the world at all.

Now let us ask the question, why is it that the ordinary healthy person has at one and the same time a feeling of the realness of the world, and of the realness of what is imaginative and personal? How did it come about that you and I are like that? It is a great advantage to be like that, because if we are we can use our imagination to make the world more exciting, and we can use the things of the real world to be imaginative about. Do we just grow like that? Well, what I am saying is that we do not grow like that, not unless at the beginning each one of us has a mother able to introduce the world to us in small doses.

Now what are children like when they are two, three, or four years old? In this particular matter of seeing the world as it is, what can we say about the toddler? For the toddler, every sensation is tremendously intense. We, as grown-ups, only at special moments reach to this wonderful intensity of feeling which belongs to the early years, and anything that helps us to get there without frightening us is welcome. For some it is music or a picture that gets us there, for some it is a football match, and for others it is dressing up for a dance, or getting a glimpse of the Queen as she passes in her car. Happy are those whose feet are well planted on the earth and yet who keep the capacity for enjoying intense sensations, even if only in the dreams that are dreamed and remembered.

For the little child, and how much more for the infant, life is just a series of terrifically intense experiences. You have noticed what happens when you interrupt play; in fact you like to give warning, so that if possible the child will be able to bring the play to some sort of an end and so tolerate your interference. A toy that an uncle gave your little boy is a bit of the real world, and yet if it is given in the right way at the right time and by the right person it has a meaning for the child which we ought to be able to understand and allow for. Perhaps we can remember a little toy that we had ourselves, and what it meant to us then. How drab it looks now if it is still on the mantelpiece! The child of two, three, and four is in two worlds at once. The world that we share with the child is also the child's own imaginative world, and so the child is able to experience it intensely. The reason for this is that we do not insist, when we are dealing with a child of that age, on an exact perception of the external world. A child's feet need not be all the time firmly planted on the earth. If a little girl wants to fly we do not just say 'Children don't fly'. Instead of that we pick her up and carry her around above our heads and put her on top of the cupboard, so that she feels to have flown like a bird to her nest.

Only too soon the child will find that flying cannot be done magically. Probably in dreams magical floating through the air may be retained to some extent, or at any rate there will be a dream about taking rather long steps. Some fairy story like the one about the Seven-League Boots, or the Magic Carpet, will be the grown-ups' contribution to this theme. At ten years or so the child will be practising long-jump and high-jump, trying to jump farther and higher than the others. That will be all that remains, except dreams, of the tremendously acute sensations associated with the idea of flying that came naturally at the age of three.

The point is that we don't clamp down reality on the little child, and we hope that we shall not have to clamp it down even when the child is five or six years old, because, if all goes well, by that age the child will have started a scientific interest in this thing that grown-ups call the real world. This real world has much to offer, as long as its acceptance does not mean a loss of the reality of the personal imaginative or inner world.

For the little child it is legitimate for the inner world to be outside as well as inside, and we therefore enter into the imaginative world of the child when we play the child's games and take part in other ways in the child's imaginative experiences.

Here is a little boy of three. He is happy, he plays all day long on his own or with other children, and he is able to sit up at table and eat like grown-up people. In the day-time he is getting quite good at knowing the difference between what we call real things and what we call the child's imagination. What is he like in the night? Well, he sleeps, and no doubt dreams. Sometimes he wakes with a piercing yell. Mother jumps out of bed and goes in and turns on the light, and makes to take the child up in her arms. Is he pleased? On the contrary; he screams, 'Go away, you witch! I want my mummy'. His dream world has spread into what we call the real world, and for twenty minutes or so the mother waits, unable to do anything, because for the child she is a witch. Suddenly he puts his arms round her neck and clings to her as if she had only just turned up, and before he is able to tell her about the broomstick he drops off to sleep, so that his mother is able to put him back in the cot and return to her own bed.

What about a seven-year-old little girl, a nice little child, who tells you that at her new school all the children are against her, and the mistress is horrid and is always picking her out, making an example of her and humiliating her? Of course you go to the school and have a talk with the teacher. I am not suggesting that all teachers are perfect; nevertheless you may find she is quite a straightforward person, and that, in fact, it distresses her that this child seems to bring troubles on herself.

Well, here again you know what children are. They are not supposed to know exactly what the world is like. They must be allowed to have what would be called delusions if we were talking about grown-ups. Probably you solve the whole problem by asking the teacher to tea. Soon you may find the child going to the other extreme, and having a very strong attachment to the teacher, even idolising her, and now fearing the other children because of the teacher's love. In the course of time the whole thing settles down.

Now, if we go earlier and look at smaller children at a nursery school it is hard to guess whether they will like their teacher from what we know about her. You might know her, and perhaps you do not think much of her. She's not attractive. She acted rather selfishly when her mother was ill, or something. What the child feels about her is not based on that sort of thing. It may be that the child becomes dependent on her, and is devoted to her, because she is reliably there and kind, and she may easily become someone who is necessary for the child's happiness and growth.

But all this comes out of the relationship that exists earlier between the mother and the infant. Here there are special conditions. The mother is sharing a specialised bit of the world with her small child, keeping that bit small enough so that the child is not muddled, yet enlarging it very gradually so that the growing capacity of the child to enjoy the world is catered for. This is one of the most important parts of her job. She does it naturally.

If we look more carefully at this we shall see that there are two things that a mother does which help here. One is that she takes the trouble to avoid coincidences. Coincidences lead to muddle. Examples would be handing a baby over to someone else's care at the same time as weaning, or introducing solids during an attack of measles, and so on. The other thing is that she is able to distinguish between fact and fantasy. This is worth looking at a bit more closely.

When the boy woke up in the night and called his mother a witch, she was quite clear that she was not a witch, and so she was contented to wait until he came round. When the next day he asked her, 'Are there really witches, mummy?' she quite easily said 'No'. At the same time she looked out a story book with a witch in it. When your little boy turns away from the milk pudding you have specially prepared with the very best ingredients, and makes a face intended to convey the idea that it is poisonous, you are not upset, because you know perfectly well that it is good. You also know that just for the moment he feels that it is poisonous. You find ways round the difficulty, and quite possibly in a few minutes the pudding will be eaten with relish. If you had been uncertain of yourself you would have got all fussed up, and would have tried to force the pudding into the child's mouth to prove to *yourself* that it was good.

In all sorts of ways your clear knowledge of what is real and what is not real helps the child, because the child is only gradually getting to the understanding that the world is not as imagined, and that imagination is not exactly like the world. Each needs the other. You know that first object your baby loves—a bit of blanket or a soft toy—for the infant this is almost part of the self, and if it is taken away or washed the result is disaster. As the baby becomes able to start throwing this and other things away (expecting them to be picked up and returned, of course), you know the time is coming when you can begin to be allowed by your infant to go away and return.

I want to get back now to the beginnings. These later things are easy if the beginning happens to go well. I would like to look at the early feeding again. You remember I was describing the way in which the mother makes her breast available (or the bottle) just as the baby is preparing to conjure up something, and then lets it disappear as the idea of it fades from the baby's mind. Do you see how in doing this she is making a good start with the introduction of the world to the baby? In nine months the mother gives about a thousand feeds, and look at all the other things she does with the same delicate adaptation to exact needs. For the lucky infant the world starts off behaving in such a way that it joins up with his imagination, and so the world is woven into the texture of the imagination, and the inner life of the baby is enriched with what is perceived in the external world.

And now let us look again at the people talking about what 'real' means. If one of them had a mother who introduced the world to him when he was a baby in the ordinary good way, as you have been introducing the world to your own baby, then he will be able to see that real means two things, and he will be able to feel both kinds of reality at once. Next to him may be another person whose mother made a mess of it all, and for whom there has to be either one kind of real, or the other kind. For this unfortunate man either the world is there and every one sees the same thing, or else everything is imaginary and personal. We can leave these two people arguing.

So a great deal depends on the way the world is presented to the infant and to the growing child. The ordinary mother can start and carry through this amazing business of introducing the world in small doses, not because she is clever, like the philosophers, but simply because of the devotion she feels for her own baby.

11

The Innate Morality of the Baby

[1949]

THE ordinary thing would be to say that this talk is about 'training'. The word 'training' certainly brings to your mind the sort of thing that I want to go into now, which is the business of how to get your baby to become nice and clean and good and obedient, sociable, moral, and everything. I was going to say happy, too, but you cannot teach a child to be happy.

This word 'training' always seems to me to be something that belongs to the care of dogs. Dogs do need to be trained. I suppose we can learn something from dogs, in that if you know your own mind your dog is happier than if you do not; and children, too, like you to have your own ideas about things. But a dog doesn't have to grow up eventually into a human being, so when we come to your baby we have to start again, and the best thing is to see how far we can leave out the word 'training' altogether.

I have several things to get out of the way before I can get down to what I really want to say. For one thing, there is the matter of your own standards. Eventually, your child has either to accept your standards or else rebel against them. Your standards are deeply founded and you would be lost without them.

But standards vary. In one block standards are different in the different flats, because one family values physical strength or manual labour, and another puts value on cleverness, and another on cleanliness, and so on. It would be absurd for any one to ask you to alter your standards just because you have a baby.

Another thing we have to remember is that every one was a baby once, and the way in which your parents brought you up is stored away somewhere in you, perhaps even remembered, and it is not easy to be free from the tendency either to repeat exactly what your parents did to you, or (if an extreme attitude was adopted by them) to go to the other extreme. I am talking chiefly to parents who have standards which are not too rigid, and for whom the words love and hate are more important than words like good, clean, beautiful, bad, and ugly.

And another thing I must get out of the way—I must admit that there are bound to be some children, even in the best homes, who are not developing quite satisfactorily. With a child who is in difficulties you may have to do what you rightly feel is not good, and adopt firm training methods which definitely cramp the spontaneity of the child, simply to make life bearable. This just cannot be helped, and it would be a good idea, on some other occasion, to discuss the management of those children who are in too much of a mess to be allowed to develop along their own lines. At present, however, I'm discussing the early stages, and what an ordinary good mother does with her infant or little child who is developing satisfactorily.

Your baby is tremendously dependent on you, at the beginning almost entirely dependent on you, but this does not mean that the baby is dependent on you for feeling good or bad. Ideas of good and bad turn up in every infant from inside. The dependence has to do with the setting that you provide to make possible the full development of the infant into a little child, and of the little child into an older child.

If I can take for granted all this about the setting you provide (bodily care, reliable behaviour, active adaptation to the baby's needs, fun, etc.) I can then go on to say that there are innate tendencies in every infant towards morality, and towards all the different kinds of good behaviour which you yourselves value. If these tendencies can be found in the infant, is it not worth while waiting for them? Eventually the child will be able to adopt your standards (in fact, your standards may prove to be too low, like when you teach him to say 'ta' when he doesn't feel grateful). But it is a complex matter, this process of development from impulsiveness and the claim to control every one and everything, to an ability to conform. I cannot tell you how complex it is. Such development takes time. Only if you feel it is worth while will you allow space and time for what has to happen.

I am still talking about infants, but it is so very difficult to describe what is happening in the first months in infant terms. To make it easier, let us look now at a boy of five or six drawing. I shall pretend he is conscious of what is going on, though he is not really. He is making a picture. What does he do? He knows the impulse to scribble and to make a mess. That is not a picture. These primitive pleasures have to be kept fresh, but at the same time he wants to express ideas, and also to express them in such a way that they may possibly be understood. If he achieves a picture he has found a series of controls that satisfy him. First of all there is a piece of paper of a particular size and shape which he accepts. Then he hopes to use a certain amount of skill that has come of practice. Then he knows that the picture when it is finished must have balance—you know, the tree on either side of the house—this is an expression of the fairness which he needs and probably gets from the parents. The points of interest must balance, and so must the lights and shades and the colour scheme. The interest of the picture must be spread over the whole paper, and yet there must be a central theme which knits the whole thing together. Within this system of accepted, indeed self-imposed, controls he tries to express an idea, and to keep some of the freshness of feeling that belonged to the idea when it was born. It almost takes my breath away to describe all this, yet your children get to it quite naturally if you will give them half a chance.

Of course, as I said, he does not know all those things in a way that would make it possible for him to talk about them. Still less does an infant know what is going on within.

The baby is rather like this older boy, only first of all it is much more obscure. The pictures don't actually get painted, in fact they are not of course pictures at all, but they are little contributions to society which only the mother of the baby is sensitive enough to appreciate. A smile can contain all this, or a clumsy gesture of the arm, or a sucking noise indicating readiness for a feed. Perhaps there is a whimpering sound by which the sensitive mother knows that if she comes quickly she may be able to attend personally to a motion which otherwise just becomes a wasted mess. This is the very beginning of co-operation and social sense, and is worth all the trouble it involves. How many children who wet the bed for some years after they could get out and save a lot of washing, are going back in the night to their infancy, trying to go over their experiences again, trying to find and correct something that was missing. The thing missing in that case was the mother's sensitive attention to signals of excitement or distress which would have enabled her to make personal and good what otherwise had to be wasted, because there was no one there to participate in what happened.

The problem is: in order eventually to have a clean and dry child are you to *train* your baby to be clean, or are you to accept the dirtiness, not mind about it, and be contented sometimes to catch these moments in which the baby is beginning to be able to communicate with you, and is beginning to be able to let you know how to adapt with success to his changing needs? You will judge according to your own inclination, and according to what kind of infant you have. But the first method is not so rich or rewarding as the second.

By the first method you feel your aim is to implant goodness, and a sense of right and wrong. But the baby is left without firm roots to the good behaviour. Over here are the baby's spontaneity and capacity to make a contribution to society, and over there, quite separately, are the world's demands. It is like inviting the baby to split into two halves. By the second method the innate tendencies towards morality are being allowed. Because of the mother's sensitive ways, which belong to the fact of her love, the roots of the infant's personal moral sense are preserved. The baby hates to waste an experience, and much prefers to wait, and bear frustration of primitive pleasures, if waiting adds the warmth of a personal relationship. Only all this does not become clear until you have acted in the way you love to act so sensitively over a period of some months, or years.

The mother who easily feels these things, and who has the courage to act according to her feelings, is actually going to have an easier time later on. She 'spoils' her infant at the beginning, except that we do not call it 'spoiling' then, because at the beginning it is natural and valuable.

And then what happens? I would say that the infant builds up within the self the idea of a mother, a mother just like you. This inside mother is then a human being who (like the infant) feels it is a happy achievement to get any experience within the orbit of a human relationship. The infant with an inside good mother is no longer completely dependent on you, and on your way of going to meet whatever turns up.

Because of these things building up within the infant, the mother becomes gradually released from the need to be so terribly sensitive. One could say that the infant comes to have a capacity to dream about a mother, and her loving care. A new thing happens now, for instead of presenting the mother in a crude way with a smile, or a motion, the baby wants to tell the mother about the dreams. The mother has to be able to be imaginative for the baby to get this across, because a little playing can mean so much, and who but the mother knows that the dreams can be happy, frightening, or sad, long before talking brings the ability to tell what has been dreamed in words.

To illustrate this I will again use our little boy making a picture. We see that he has gone a stage further. He is long past scribbling, and he has now got beyond drawing a picture; now he has the picture (or dream) within himself before actually attempting to put it on to paper. He now chooses the paper according to the picture he has in mind.

Very soon, therefore, if the mother has been able to be as sensitive as the infant at the beginning, she finds that the primitive gratifications which the baby needs are being experienced in the baby's own rapidly developing inner world, and therefore there is less and less dependence on her exact adaptation to the infant's needs in real life. There is less and less need in the baby, then, for actual greediness, and actual messing, and actual control over things.

So, civilisation has started again inside a new human being. In practice, when all goes well, you will be neither training nor neglecting your infant. You will be providing a reliable setting in which the infant can sooner or later discover an interest in co-operating with you, an interest in seeing your point of view, liking to do what you like, and being pleased to adopt your ideas of right and wrong. Such an infant will soon be playing the part of good mother with a doll. Don't be surprised if you find the doll being severely punished for making a mess. Little children are fiercely moral. It is for you to catch on to their primitive morality and to tone it down gradually to the humanity that comes from mature understanding.

12

Weaning

[1949]

You know me well enough by now not to expect me to tell you exactly how and when to wean; there are more good methods than one, and you can get advice from your Health Visitor or clinic. What I want to do is to talk about weaning in a general way, to help you to see what you are doing, whichever way exactly you do it.

The fact is that most mothers don't have any difficulty. Why is this?

The main thing is that the feeding itself has gone well. The baby really has had something to be weaned from. You cannot deprive people of something they have never had. Some of you may remember things we had before the war, or when we were children, which we rather took for granted. On the whole it was those who had enjoyed them who best gave them up. The shortages were very difficult for those who had not had quite enough already. Those coming later, and who had never known these things, did not miss them.

I can distinctly remember on one occasion, as a little boy, being allowed to eat as much of raspberries and cream as I could possibly take. It was a wonderful experience. Now I can enjoy memories of that one experience better than I enjoy eating raspberries. Perhaps you can remember something like that?

So the basis of weaning is the good feeding experience. In an ordinary nine months at the breast a baby has had it a thousand or so times, and this gives plenty of good memories, or material for good dreams. But it is not the thousand times, it is also the way the baby and the mother were brought together. The mother's sensitive adaptation (as I have said so often) to the infant's needs started off the idea of the world as a good place. The world went to meet the infant, and so the infant could go out to meet the world. The mother's co-operation with the baby at the beginning led naturally on to the baby's co-operation with the mother.

If you believe, as I do, that the baby has ideas right from the start, the feeding times were often pretty terrible, disrupting the quiet of sleep or of waking contemplation. Instinctual demands can be fierce and frightening, and at first can seem to the infant like threats to existence. Being hungry is like being possessed by wolves.

By nine months the baby has become used to this sort of thing, and has become able to hold together even while these instinctual urges hold sway. The baby has even become able to acknowledge the urges as a part of what it means to be a person alive.

As we look at the infant developing into a person, we can see how the mother is gradually perceived in the quiet times as a person too, as something attractive and valued exactly as she appears. How awful then to be hungry, and to feel oneself ruthlessly attacking this same mother. No wonder infants often lose appetite. No wonder some infants fail to allow the breasts to the mother, but separate off the mother who is loved as whole and beautiful from the things (the breasts) that are the objects of excited attack.

Adults find it difficult to let themselves go when they are excited about each other, and this causes much misery, and makes for unsuccessful marriages. The basis for eventual health in this, and in many other respects, is the whole experience of being carried through infancy by the ordinary good mother who is not afraid of her infant's ideas, and who loves it when her baby goes at her all out.

Perhaps you see why it really is a richer experience for a mother to feed by the breast, and for a baby to be fed at the breast? Everything can be done as well by bottle, and often it is best to go on to the bottle, which may be easier for the baby precisely because it is less exciting. But the breast-feeding experience carried through and terminated successfully is a good basis for life. It provides rich dreams, and makes people able to take risks.

But all good things must come to an end, as the saying is. It is part of the good thing that it ends.

Do you remember the baby I described who caught hold of a spoon? He took it, he mouthed it, he enjoyed having it to play with, and then he dropped it. So the idea of the ending can come from the baby.

It is plain that at seven to eight to nine months a baby is beginning to be able to play games of throwing things away. It is a very important game, and it can even be exasperating, because someone has to be all the time bringing back the things thrown down. Even in the street, when you come out of the shop you find the baby has thrown out of the pram on to the pavement a teddy bear, two gloves, a pillow, three potatoes, and a piece of soap. Probably you find someone picking everything up, because the baby obviously expects this.

Well, by nine months most babies are pretty clear about getting rid of things. They may even wean themselves.

In weaning, the aim really is to use the baby's developing ability to get rid of things, and to let the loss of the breast be not just simply a chance affair.

But we must look to see why a baby should ever be weaned at all. Why not go on for ever? Well, I think I have to say that it would be sentimental never to wean. It would be unreal somehow. A wish to wean must come from the mother. She must be brave enough to stand the baby's anger and the awful ideas that go with anger, and just to do what rounds off the job of good feeding. No doubt the baby who has been successfully fed is happy to be weaned in due course, especially as there goes with this a vast extension of the field of experience.

Naturally, when weaning-time comes, you will be already introducing other things. You will have provided hard things, rusks and so on, for the baby to chew, and you will have substituted broth or something for one of the breast feeds. You will have put up with a possible refusal of anything new, and found that, by waiting and then going back to the thing that had been refused, you may be rewarded by an acceptance of it. There is usually no need for a sudden change-over from all breast to no breast at all. When (through illness or some other bad chance) the sudden change-over has had to be made, you will have expected difficulties.

If you know that the reactions to weaning are complex you will naturally avoid handing your baby over to someone else's care just as you wean. It would be a pity to wean at the same time as you move from one home to another, or when you go to stay with your aunt. Weaning is one of those experiences that the baby can grow on, if you provide a stable setting for the experience. If you cannot do this, then weaning can be a time when difficulties start.

Another thing, you may easily find that your baby thrives on being weaned in the day, but perhaps for the last feed the breast is the only good thing. You see, your baby is growing up, but his forward march is not maintained all the time. You will find this all along. You will be quite happy if your child is as old as his age some of the time; perhaps he will be beyond his age at certain moments. But every now and again he will be just a baby, even a tiny baby. And you go to meet these changes.

Your boy is dressing up and bravely fighting enemies. He is ordering every one about. He bumps his head on the table as he stands up and then suddenly he is a baby, with his head on your lap, sobbing. You expect this, and you expect your baby of twelve months to be only six months old at times. It is all part of your skilled job, knowing just how old your child is at any one moment.

So you may be going on with a breast feed in the evening after you have weaned in the day. But sooner or later you will have to wean altogether, and if you know what you intend to do it is easier for the child than if you cannot make up your mind.

Let me look and see now what reactions you may expect to the weaning which you so bravely do. It may be, as I have said, that the baby does a self-weaning act, and so you do not notice any trouble. Even here there may be some lessening of the zest for food.

Very often, when the weaning is done it is done gradually, and in a stable setting, and no special trouble arises. The infant obviously loves to have the new experience. But I do not want you to think it is very unusual if there are reactions to weaning, even severe ones. A baby who has been doing well may react by losing eagerness for food, or by painfully refusing food, showing a longing for it by irritability and crying. It would be harmful to force food on the baby at this stage. For the time being everything has gone bad from his point of view and you cannot get round this. You can only wait, being ready for a gradual return of feeding.

Or the baby may start to wake screaming. You just help on the waking-up process. Or things may go well, but nevertheless you notice a change towards sadness in the child, a new note in the crying, perhaps going over into a musical note. This sadness is not necessarily bad. Don't just think sad babies need to be jogged up and down till they smile. They have something to be sad about, and sadness comes to an end if you leave it.

The baby is sad at times like the weaning-time because circumstances have made anger come and spoil something that was good. In the baby's dreams the breasts are no longer good, they have been hated, and so now they are felt to be bad, even dangerous. That is why where is a place for the wicked woman in the fairy stories who gives poisoned apples. For the newly-weaned infant it is the really good mother whose breasts have become bad, and so there has to be time allowed for recovery and readjustment. But an ordinary good mother does not shirk even this. Often in the twenty-four hours she has to be the bad mother for a few minutes, and she gets used to this. In time she is seen as the good mother again. Eventually the child grows up and gets to know her just as she really is, neither ideal nor indeed a witch.

Yes, there is a wider aspect of weaning—weaning is not only getting a baby to take other foods, or to use a cup, or to feed actively using the hands. It includes the gradual process of disillusionment, which is part of the parents' task.

The ordinary good mother and father do not want to be worshipped by their children. They endure the extremes of being idealised and hated, hoping that eventually their children will see them as the ordinary human beings they certainly are.

13

Knowing and Learning

[1950]

THERE is much for a young mother to learn. She gets told useful things by experts, about the introduction of solids into the diet, about vitamins, and about the use of the weight chart: and then sometimes she gets told about quite a different kind of thing, for instance, about her reaction to her infant's refusal of food.

It seems to me to be important for you to be quite clear about the difference between these two types of knowledge. What you do and know, simply by virtue of the fact that you are the mother of an infant, is as far apart from what you know by learning as is the east from the west coast of England. I cannot put this too strongly. Just as the professor who found out about the vitamins that prevent rickets really has something to teach you, so you really have something to teach him about the other kind of knowledge, that which comes to you naturally.

The mother who breast-feeds her baby simply does not have to bother about fats and proteins while she is thoroughly caught up in the management of the early stages. By the time she weans at nine months or so and the baby is making fewer demands on her, she is becoming free to study facts and advice which doctors and nurses offer. Obviously there is a great deal that she could not know intuitively, and she does want to be told about the giving of solids, and about how to use the sort of foods that are available in such a way that the baby will be able to grow and keep healthy. But she must wait for such instruction until she is in a state of mind to receive it.

We can easily see that years of brilliant research have gone into the doctor's bit of advice about vitamins, and we can look with awe at the scientist's work and at the self-discipline that such work entails, and be grateful when, by the results of scientific research, a great deal of suffering can be avoided, perhaps by some quite simple advice like adding a few drops of cod-liver oil to the diet.

At the same time the scientist, if he cares to do so, may look with awe at the mother's intuitive understanding, which makes her able to care for her infant without learning. In fact, the essential richness of this intuitive understanding, I would say, is that it *is* natural and unspoiled by learning.

The difficult task, in preparing a series of talks and books on infant care, is to know how to avoid disturbance of what comes naturally to mothers while getting them informed accurately as to the useful facts that emerge from scientific research.

I want you to be able to feel confident about your capacity as mothers, and not feel that because you could not know about vitamins, you also could not know about, for instance, how to hold your infant.

How to hold your infant; that would be a good example for me to follow up.

The phrase 'holding the baby' has a definite meaning in the English language; someone was co-operating with you over something, and then waltzed off, and you were left 'holding the baby'. By this we can see that everybody knows that mothers naturally have a sense of responsibility, and if they have a baby in their arms they are involved in some special way. Of course, some women get left holding the baby literally, in the sense that the father is unable to enjoy the part he has to play, and unable to share with the mother the great responsibility which a baby must always be to someone.

Or perhaps there is no father. Ordinarily, however, the mother feels supported by her husband and so is free to be a mother properly, and when she holds her baby she does it naturally, and without thinking it out. Such a mother will be surprised if I talk about such a thing as holding a baby as a skilled job.

When people see a baby they love to be able to be allowed to experience just this thing, of holding the baby in their arms. You don't let people hold your baby if you feel it means nothing to them. Babies are very sensitive indeed to the way they are held, so that they cry with one person and rest contented with another, even when they are quite tiny. Sometimes a little girl will ask to hold a newly-arrived baby brother or sister, and this is a big event. The wise mother will remember not to give the child the whole responsibility, and will be there all the time if she lets this happen, ready to take the baby back into her own safe keeping. The wise mother will certainly not just take it for granted that an older sister is safe with the baby in her arms. This would be to deny the meaning of it all. I know people who can remember throughout their lives the awful feeling of holding the baby brother or sister, and of the nightmare of not feeling safe. In the nightmare the baby is dropped. The fear which can turn up in the nightmare as doing harm in practice makes the big sister catch hold of the baby too tightly.

All this leads on to what you do yourself quite naturally because of your devotion to your baby. You are not anxious and so are not gripping too tight. You are not afraid you will throw the baby on to the floor. You just adapt the pressure of your arms to the baby's needs, and you move slightly, and you perhaps make some sounds. The baby feels you breathing. There is warmth that comes from your breath and your skin, and the baby finds your holding to be good.

Of course there are all kinds of mothers, and there are some who are not quite so happy about the way they hold their babies. Some feel a bit doubtful; the baby seems happier in the cot. There may be something left over in such a mother of the fear which she had to deal with when she was a little girl, when her mother let her hold a new-born baby. Or she may have had a mother who was not very good at this sort of thing herself, and she is afraid of passing on to her baby some uncertainty belonging to the past. An anxious mother uses the cot as much as possible, or even hands the baby over to the care of a nurse, carefully chosen because of the natural way she handles babies. There is room for all kinds of mothers in the world, and some will be good at one thing and some good at another. Or shall I say some will be bad at one thing and some bad at another? Some are anxious holders.

It may be worth while looking even a little more closely at this business, because if you do handle your baby well I want you to be able to know that you are doing something of importance. This is a little part of the way in which you give a good foundation for the mental health of this new member of the community.

Look at it imaginatively.

Here is the infant right at the beginning (from what happens at the beginning we can see what happens, over and over again, later on). Let me describe three stages in the infant's relation to the world (represented by your arms and your breathing body), leaving out hunger and anger, and all the great upheavals. First stage: the infant is self-contained, a live creature, yet surrounded by space. The infant knows of nothing, except of self. Second stage: the infant moves an elbow, a knee, or straightens out a little. The space has been crossed. The infant has surprised the environment. Third stage: you who are holding the infant jump a little, because the door bell rang, or the kettle boiled over, and again the space has been crossed. This time the environment has surprised the infant.

First, the self-contained infant is in the space that is maintained between the child and the world, then the infant surprises the world, and thirdly, the world surprises the infant. This is so simple that I think it will appeal to you as a natural sequence, and therefore a good basis for the study of the way you hold your infant.

This is all very obvious, but the trouble is that if you do not know these things you may easily let your immense skill get wasted, because you will not see how to explain to neighbours, and to your husband, how necessary it is for you, in your turn, to have a space to yourself in which you can start your infant off with a sound basis for life.

Let me put it this way. The baby in the space becomes ready, in the course of time, for the movement that surprises the world, and the infant who has found the world in this way becomes, in time, ready to welcome the surprises that the world has in store.

The baby does not know that the space around is maintained by you. How careful you are that the world shall not impinge before the infant has found it! By a live and breathing quietness you follow the life in the infant with the life in yourself, and you wait for the gestures that come from the infant, gestures that lead to your being discovered.

If you feel heavy with sleep, and especially if you are in a depressed mood, you put the infant in a cot, because you know that your sleeping state is not alive enough to keep going the infant's idea of a space around.

If I have referred specially to tiny infants, and your management of them, this does not mean that I am not also referring to older children. Of course most of the time the older child has passed through to a much more complex state of affairs, and is not in need of the very special management which comes naturally to you when you are holding your baby who is only a few hours old. But how often it happens that the older child, just for a few minutes, or for an hour or two, needs to go back, and to go over the ground again that belongs to the earliest stages. Perhaps your child has had an accident, and comes to you crying. It may be five or ten minutes before there is a return to play. In the meantime you have had the child in your arms, and you have allowed for just this same sequence that I have been talking about. First of all, the quiet yet live holding, and then the readiness for the child to move and to find you, as the tears clear away. And at length you are able, quite naturally, to put the child down. Or a child is unwell, or sad, or tired. Whatever it is, for a little while the child is an infant, and you know that time has to be given so that there can be a natural return from essential security to ordinary conditions.

Of course I might have chosen many other examples of the way in which you have knowledge, simply because you are specialists in this particular matter of the care of your own children. I want to encourage you to keep and defend this specialist knowledge. It cannot be taught. Then you can learn things from other kinds of specialist. Only if you can keep what is natural in you is it safe for you to learn anything that doctors and nurses can teach you.

It might be thought that I have been trying to teach you now how to hold your baby. This seems to me to be far from the truth. I am trying to describe various aspects of the things you do naturally, in order that you may be able to recognise what you do, and in order that you may be able to get the feeling of your natural capacity. This is important, because unthinking people will often try to teach you how to do the things which you can *do* better than you can be *taught* to do them. If you are sure of all this, you can start to add to your value as a mother by learning the things that can be taught, for the best of our civilisation and culture offers much that is of value, if you can take it without the loss of what comes to you naturally.

14

Instincts and Normal Difficulties

[1950]

When it comes to illness, talks and books are rather misleading. What a mother needs for her ill child is a doctor who can see and examine the baby and have a discussion with her. But the common troubles of ordinary healthy children are a different matter, and I think mothers find it rather helpful when it is pointed out to them that their well children are not to be expected to go straight ahead without giving any cause for worry and anxiety.

Ordinary healthy children undoubtedly do present all kinds of symptoms.

What is it that causes these troubles in infancy and early childhood? If we take it for granted that your management has been skilled and consistent, so that you can be said to have laid down the foundations for the health of this new member of society satisfactorily, what is it that determines that the child still presents problems? The answer is, I think, chiefly to do with the matter of instincts. It is about this that I wish to write now.

It may be that just for the moment your child is lying quietly over there sleeping, or cuddling something, or playing, in one of those quiet periods that you welcome. But you know only too well that in health there are recurring excitements. You can either look at it one way and say that the child gets hungry, that the body has needs, or instincts, or else you look at it another way, and say that the child begins to have exciting ideas. These exciting experiences play a very important part in the child's development, promoting as well as complicating growth.

During excitement the child has impelling needs. Often you are able to satisfy them. The needs, however, can be very great indeed, at certain moments, and some of them cannot be satisfied fully.

Now, some of these needs are universally recognised and easy to bring to your notice, whereas others are difficult to describe without causing surprise and even alarm. It is easy to talk about hunger in general, because this is something which is quite respectable; the trouble is how to talk about the other kinds of excitements.

The fact is that any part of the body may be excited at one time or another. The skin, for instance. You have seen children scratching their faces, or scratching the skin in other places, the skin itself becoming excited, and developing some kind of rash. And there are certain parts of the skin that are more sensitive than others, especially at certain times. You can go over the whole of the body of the child and think out the various ways in which excitement becomes localised. We certainly cannot leave out the sexual parts. I can assure you that all these things are very important to the infant, and they make up the high lights of the waking life of infancy. Exciting ideas go along with the bodily excitements, and you will not be surprised if I say that these ideas not only have to do with pleasure, they also have to do with love, if the baby is developing well. Gradually the infant becomes a person capable of loving persons, and feeling loved as a person. There is a very powerful bond between the baby and the mother and father and other people around, and the excitements have to do with this love. In the form of some bodily excitement, love periodically becomes acutely felt.

The ideas that go with the primitive love impulses are predominantly destructive, and are nearly related to those of anger. The result for the baby feels good, however, if the activity leads to instinctual gratifications.

You can easily see that during such periods there is inevitably a great deal of frustration, and this leads in health to anger, even rage. You will not think your infant is ill if from time to time you are presented with a picture of rage, which you learn to distinguish from sadness, fear, and pain. In rage the infant's heart is beating faster than it will ever beat again. In fact, as many as 220 heart beats a minute can be counted, if you want to listen. Anger means that the child has got as far as believing in something and in someone to be angry with.

Now, a risk is taken whenever emotions are fully felt, and these experiences of excitement and rage must often be very painful; so you will find your perfectly normal child trying to find ways of avoiding the most intense feelings. By one way in which feelings are avoided there is a damping down of instinct—for instance, the infant becomes unable to let the full extent of the excitement of feeding take place. By another, a child accepts certain kinds of food but not other kinds. Or other people may give the feed, but not the mother. Every possible variation can be found, if one knows enough children. This is not necessarily illness; it is simply that we see little children discovering all sorts of techniques for managing feelings which are intolerable. They have to avoid a certain amount of natural feelings because these are too intense, or else because the full experience brings about painful conflicts.

Feeding difficulties are common in normal children, and it often happens that mothers have to put up with very disappointing months, and even years, in which a child wastes all their ability to provide good food. Perhaps a child only takes routine food, and anything prepared with special care or delicacy is rejected. Sometimes mothers have to let children refuse food altogether for quite a long time, for if they try to force it in such circumstances they only increase the child's resistance. If they wait, however, and do not make a 'thing' out of it, at some time or other the child will start eating again. One can well imagine a mother who is not experienced being worried during such a period, and needing a doctor or a nurse to reasssure her that she is not neglecting her child, or doing harm.

Now, as I have said, it is possible to discuss hunger, but it is more difficult to discuss the other excitements. But mothers want to have everything mentioned, they cannot afford to have blind spots in the care of their infants. The fact is that infants periodically have various kinds of orgies (not only feeding orgies), and these orgies are natural, and very important to them. Their excretory processes are particularly exciting to them, and the sexual parts of their bodies even more so, at appropriate moments, as they grow.

By the way, you will have noticed that babies do not start off thinking the same as you do about what is nice and what is nasty. Stuff that is got rid of with excitement and pleasure is likely to be felt to be good, and even good to eat, and good to smear the cot and the walls with. That may be a nuisance, but it is natural, and you will not mind too much. You will be contented to wait for more civilised sentiments to turn up of their own accord. Sooner or later disgust turns up, and, even quite suddenly, a baby who was eating soap and drinking bathwater will become prudish, and go off any kind of food that even looks like excretions, which were (till a few days previously) handled and pushed into the mouth.

Sometimes we see a return to the infant state in older children, and then we know that some difficulty has blocked the way to progress, and the child has a need to go back over the ground covered in infancy, in order to re-establish the rights of infants and the laws of natural development.

Mothers watch these things happening, and, as mothers, they do indeed play a part in it all; but they would rather watch a steady and natural developmental process than impose their own ideas of right and wrong.

One trouble that comes from trying to impose a pattern of right and wrong on an infant is that the infant's instincts come along and spoil it all. The moments of acute experience break down the baby's efforts to gain love through compliance. The result then is that he or she becomes upset, instead of strengthened, by the operation of the instincts.

The normal child has not too severely squashed the powerful instinctual feelings back, and is therefore subject to disturbances, and these look like symptoms to the ignorant observer. I have mentioned rage; temper tantrums and periods of absolute defiance are usual at two and three. Nightmares are frequently experienced by little children, and by the piercing yells at midnight the neighbours wonder what you are up to.

And what a lot of children stammer a little at two, three, and four, without ever developing into stutterers. They simply need you to pay more attention to them when they have some very important thing to say. They feel we ought to know what they mean without all this palaver of speech, and they feel they have rights over people, who are only gradually perceived as having rights of their own.

At this early age children do not have to be ill to be frightened of dogs, doctors, and the dark, or to be imaginative about sounds and shadows, and vague shapes in the twilight; and they do not have to be ill to be liable to colic, or to sickness, or to going green when they are excited about something; they do not have to be ill to refuse to have anything to do with an adored father for a week or two, or to refuse to say 'ta' to an aunt; and they do not have to be ill to want to put the new sister in the dustbin, or to be rather cruel to the cat in a big effort to avoid hating the new baby.

And you know all about the way clean children become dirty, and dry ones wet, and how, in fact, in the period from two to five almost anything can happen. Put it all down to the workings of the instincts, and to the terrific feelings that belong to the instincts, and (since with all bodily happenings there are ideas) to the painful conflicts that result from all this in the child's imagination. Let me add that at this critical age the instincts are no longer just infantile in quality, and in describing them we do not say enough if we keep to the nursery terms, such as 'greediness' and 'messing'. When a healthy three-year-old child says 'I love you' there is meaning in it like that between men and women who love, and who are in love. It can, in fact, be sexual in the ordinary sense, involving the bodily sex parts, and including ideas that are like those of adolescents or adults in love. Tremendous forces are at work, yet all you need to do is to keep the home together, and to expect anything. Relief will come through the operation of time. When the child is five or six, things will then sober down a lot, and will stay sobered down till puberty, so you will have an easier few years, during which you can hand part of the responsibility and part of the task over to the schools, and to the trained teachers.

PART II

Family Affairs

1

What About Father?

[1944]

IN my job many mothers have discussed with me the question: What about father? I suppose it is clear to every one that, in normal times, it depends on what mother does about it whether father does or does not get to know his baby. There are all sorts of reasons why it is difficult for a father to take part in his infant's upbringing. For one thing he may be scarcely ever at home when the baby is awake. But very often, even when father is home, mother finds it a little difficult to know when to make use of her husband, and when to wish him out of the way. No doubt it is often far simpler to get the baby to bed before father comes home, just as it is a good idea to get the washing done and the food cooked. But many of you will agree from your experience that it is a great help in the relation between married people when they share day by day the little details of experience in the care of their infant, little details which seem silly to outsiders, but which are tremendously important at the time both to the parents and to the infant. And as the infant grows into a toddler and into a little child, the richness of detail increases and with this the bond between father and mother can become even deeper.

I know that some fathers are very shy about their babies at the beginning, and no doubt some can never be brought to be interested in infants; but, at any rate, mothers can get their husbands to help in little things, and can arrange for the baby to be bathed when father can watch, and even take part if he wants to. As I have said, it depends quite a lot on what you do about it.

One could not assume in every case that it is a good thing for father to come early into the picture. People are so different from each other. Some men feel as if they would be better mothers than their wives are, and they can be quite a nuisance. This is specially true when they are able to waltz in and be very patient 'mothers' for about half an hour and then waltz out again, ignoring the fact that mothers have to be good mothers twenty-four hours a day, day in and day out. And then it may be that there are some fathers who really would make better mothers than their wives, but still they cannot be mothers; so some way out of the difficulty has to be found, other than by just letting mother fade out of the picture. But usually mothers know they are good at their own job, and then they can let their husbands into the picture if they wish.

If we start at the beginning we can see that the infant first of all knows mother. Sooner or later certain qualities of mother are recognised by the infant, and some of these one associates always with mother—softness, sweetness. But mother has all sorts of stern qualities as well; for instance, she can be hard, severe, and strict; indeed, her punctuality about feeds is valued tremendously by the infant as soon as he can accept the fact that he cannot be fed just exactly when he wants to feed. I would say that certain qualities of mother that are not essentially part of her gradually group together in the infant's mind, and these qualities draw to themselves the feelings which the infant at length becomes willing to have towards father. How much better a strong father who can be respected and loved than just qualities of mother, rules and regulations, permits and prohibitions, things dead and uncompromising.

So when father comes into the child's life as a father, he takes over feelings that the infant has already had towards certain properties of mother, and it is a great relief to mother when father can take over in this way.

Let me see if I can separate out the different ways in which father is valuable. The first thing I want to say is that father is needed at home to help mother to feel well in her body and happy in her mind. A child is very sensitive indeed to the relationship between the parents, and if all goes well off-stage, so to speak, the child is the first to appreciate the fact, and tends to show this appreciation by finding life easier, and by being more contented and more easy to manage. I suppose this is what an infant or a child would mean by 'social security'.

The union of father and mother provides a fact, a hard fact around which the child may build a fantasy, a rock to which he can cling and against which he can kick; and furthermore it provides part of the natural foundation for a personal solution to the problem of the triangular relationship.

The second thing, as I have said, is that father is needed to give mother moral support, to be the backing for her authority, to be the human being who stands for the law and order which mother plants in the life of the child. He does not have to be there all the time to do this, but he has to turn up often enough for the child to feel that he is real and alive. Much of the arranging of a child's life must be done by mother, and children like to feel that mother can manage the home when father is not actually in it. Yes, indeed, every woman has to be able to speak and act with authority; but if she has to be the whole thing, and has to provide the whole of the strong or strict element in her children's lives as well as the love, she carries a big burden indeed. Besides, it is much easier for the children to be able to have two parents; one parent can be felt to remain loving while the other is being hated, and this in itself has a stabilising influence. Sometimes you see a child hitting or kicking his mother, and you feel that if her husband were backing her up the child would probably want to kick him, and very likely he would not try it on. Every now and again the child is going to hate someone, and if father is not there to tell him where to get off, he will hate his mother, and this will make him confused, because it is his mother that he most fundamentally loves.

The third thing to say is that father is needed by the child because of his positive qualities and the things that distinguish him from other men, and the liveliness of his personality. During the early period of life, when impressions are so vivid, then is the time for a little boy or girl to get to know father, if this is possible. Of course, I'm not asking fathers to force themselves and their personalities on their children. One child will look round for father when a few months old, reach out to him when he comes into the room, and listen for his footsteps, whereas another will turn away from him, or only very gradually allow him to become an important person in his or her life. One child will want to know what he is really like, whereas another will use father as someone to dream about, hardly getting to know him at all as others know him. Nevertheless, if father is there and wants to get to know his own child, the child is fortunate, and in the happiest circumstances father vastly enriches his child's world. When both mother and father easily accept responsibility for the child's existence the stage is set for a good home.

It is hardly possible to begin to describe the ways in which a father enriches the life of his children, so wide are the possibilities. The children form their ideal, at least in part, on what they see, or think they see, when they look at him. They get a new world opened up to them when father gradually discloses the nature of the work to which he goes in the morning, and from which he returns at night.

In the children's play there is the game 'Mothers and Fathers' and, as you know, father goes off in the morning to work, while mother does the housework and minds the children. Housework is something that children easily get to know because it is always going on around them, but the work that father does, to say nothing of his hobbies when he is off duty, widens the children's view of the world. How happy the children of a skilled craftsman who, when he is at home, is not above letting the children see the skill of his hands, and share in the making of beautiful and useful things. And if father sometimes joins in their play, he is bound to bring valuable new elements that can be woven into the playing. Moreover, father's knowledge of the world enables him to see when certain kinds of toys or apparatus would help the children in their play without hindering the natural development of their imagination. Some fathers, unfortunately, spoil it when they buy their little boy a steam engine, by playing with it themselves, or else by being so fond of it that they cannot let the child use it and perhaps break it. This is carrying father's play too far.

One of the things that father does for his children is to be alive and to stay alive during the children's early years. The value of this simple act is liable to be forgotten. Although it is natural for children to idealise their fathers, it is also very valuable for them to have the experience of living with them and getting to know them as human beings, even to the extent of finding them out. I know of a boy and girl who thought they were having a lovely time in the last war when their father was in the army. They lived with their mother in a house with a nice garden, and had everything that was necessary, and even more. Sometimes they worked up into a state of organised anti-social activity and nearly broke the house up. Now, as they look back, they can see that these periodical outbursts were attempts, unconscious at the time, to make father appear in person. However, mother managed to see them through supported by letters from her husband; but you can imagine how much she longed to have him home with her, so that she could occasionally lean back while he told the children to go to bed.

To take an extreme case: I knew a girl whose father died before she was born. The tragedy here was that she had only an idealised father on whom to base her view of man. She had not had the experience of being let down gently by a real father. In her life she easily imagined men to be ideal, which at first had the effect of bringing out the best in them. But sooner or later, inevitably, each man she got to know showed imperfections, and each time this happened she was thrown into a state of despair and was continually complaining. As you can imagine, this pattern ruined her life. How much happier she would have been if her father had been alive during her childhood, to be felt by her to be ideal, but also to be found by her to have shortcomings, and to have survived her hate of him when he disappointed her.

It is well known that there is sometimes an especially vital bond between a father and his daughter. As a matter of fact, every little girl has it in her to dream of being in mother's place, or at any rate to dream romantically. Mothers have to be very understanding when this sort of feeling is going on. Some mothers find it much easier to stand the friendship between father and son than between father and daughter. Yet it is a great pity if the close bond between father and daughter is interfered with by feelings of jealousy and rivalry, instead of being allowed to develop naturally; for sooner or later the little girl will realise the frustration that belongs to this kind of romantic attachment, and she will eventually grow up and look in other directions for the practical outcome to her imaginings. If father and mother are happy in relation to each other, these strong attachments between a father and his children will not be thought of as rivalling the greater thing, the attachment between the parents. Brothers are a great help here, providing a stepping-stone from fathers and uncles to men in general.

It is also well known that a boy and his father may find themselves at times in a state of rivalry over mother. This need give rise to no anxiety if mother and father are happy together. It need never, of course, interfere with the relationship between two parents who feel secure in each other's love. The little boy's feelings are of the strongest possible order so they should be taken seriously.

One does hear of children who never once in the whole of their childhood had father alone to themselves for a whole day, or even half a day. This seems to me to be terrible. I should say that it is mother's responsibility to send father and daughter, or father and son, out together for an expedition every now and again. This gesture will always be fully appreciated by all concerned, and some of these experiences will be treasured throughout a lifetime. It is not always easy for a mother to send her little girl out with father when she would love to go out herself with him alone; and, of course, she should go out with father alone as well, or else she will not only build up resentment in herself, but she will also be liable to lose touch with her man. But sometimes, if she can send father out with the children, or with one of them, she will be adding a great deal to her value as a mother and wife.

So if your husband is home, you may easily find that it is worth taking a lot of trouble to help him and the children to get to know each other. It is not in your power to make their relationship a rich one; that depends on father and the children. But it is very much in your power to make such a relationship possible, or to prevent it, or to mar it.

2

Their Standards and Yours

[1944]

I SUPPOSE all people have ideals and standards. Every one who is building a home has ideas about the way things should look, and about the colour scheme, and about the furniture and the way the table is laid for breakfast. Most people know just what sort of a house they would have if their ship came in, and whether they feel it is good to live in town or country, and what sort of a film it is worth while going to see.

When you got married you felt—now I can live as I like.

A little girl of five who was collecting words had heard someone say, 'The dog went home of his own accord', so she adopted the word. Next day she said to me, 'To-day's my birthday, so everything has to be my accord'. Well, when you married you felt: now at last I can live in an atmosphere which is my own accord, to use the language of the little girl. Mind you, it isn't that your accord is necessarily better than your mother-in-law's, but it is yours, and that makes all the difference.

Assuming that you got your own rooms or flat or house, you straightway proceeded to arrange and decorate in the way you felt like doing. And when you had put up the new curtains you asked people in to see your home. The point is that you had achieved a state of affairs in which your surroundings expressed you yourself, and you may have surprised even yourself by the way you did things. Evidently you had been practising for this all your life.

You were lucky in those early days if you escaped some squabbles with your husband over details. The funny thing is that arguments nearly always start about whether this or that is 'good' or 'bad', whereas the real trouble is a clash of accords, as the little girl might have said. This carpet is good for you if you bought it, or chose it, or bargained for it at a sale, and it is good from your husband's point of view if he chose it; but how can you both feel you chose it? Fortunately people who are in love do often find it possible to let their 'accords' overlap to some extent, for a while, so that is all right for a bit; and one way out of the difficulty is for it to be agreed, perhaps without anything being actually said, that the wife runs the home her way while the man has his own way at work. Every one knows that the Englishman's home is his wife's castle. And in his home a man likes to see his wife in charge, identified with the home. Alas, all too often the man has nothing in his work corresponding to his wife's independence in her own home. Too seldom does a man feel identified with his job, and this state of affairs has been getting worse as craftsmen and small shopkeepers and small men generally have been tending to become swamped out.

Talk about women not wanting to be housewives seems to me to be just nonsense, because nowhere else but in her own home is a woman in such command. Only in her own home is she free, if she has the courage, to spread herself, to find her whole self. The great thing is that she should really be able to get a flat or a house when she marries, so that she can move her elbows without brushing up against her near relations, and without bruising her own mother.

I have said all this because I want to show how difficult it must always be when a baby comes along wanting his own way, as babies do. By wanting his own way the baby is upsetting the apple-cart, and no one should say it does not matter if it does get upset. The apple-cart is the young mother's newly-found independence of spirit and newly-won respect for what she does of her own accord. Some women prefer to have no children, because marriage would seem to lose a great deal of its value for them if it did not mean the establishment of their own personal sphere of influence, won at last after years of waiting and planning.

Well, supposing that a young wife has just managed to arrange her own household and that she is proud of having done this, and that she is only just beginning to discover what she is like when she is captain of her own fate. What happens when she has a little child? I think that when she was pregnant she did not necessarily allow herself to think of the infant as a threat to her newly-found independence, because at that time there was so much else to think about. There is so much about the idea of having a baby that is exciting, interesting, and inspiring, and in any case she may have felt that the infant could be brought up to fit into her scheme of things and to enjoy growing up within her sphere of influence. So far so good, and no doubt she was right in thinking that her infant would take some of his pattern of culture and behaviour from the home he was born into. However, there is more to be said, and it is quite important.

The truth is (according to my idea) that almost from the start the new baby has his own ideas; and if you have ten children you will not find two alike although they all grow up in the same home—your household. Ten children will see ten different mothers in you, and even one child will sometimes look your way and see you as loving and beautiful, but suddenly for a few moments when the light is not good, or perhaps in the night when you go into his room because he is having a nightmare, he will see you as a dragon or a witch, or something else that is terrible and dangerous.

The point is that each new child coming into your house brings with him his own view of the world and a need to control his little bit of the world, and therefore each new child is a threat to your own set-up, your carefully constructed and well-maintained order of things. And knowing how much you value having your own way I am sorry for you.

Let me see if I can help. I think some of the difficulties that arise in this situation come from the fact that you tend to think that you like what you like because it is right, good and proper, best, cleverest, safest, quickest, most economical, and so on. No doubt you are often justified in so thinking and a child can scarcely vie with you when it comes to a matter of skill and knowledge of the world. But the main point is that it is not because your way is best—it is because it is yours that you like it and trust it. That is the real reason why you want to dominate, and why shouldn't you? The house is yours, and that is why you married—partly. Besides, you may only feel safe when you have all the strings in your own hands.

Yes, you have every right to ask people in your own house to conform to your standards, to lay the breakfast things the way you have decided, grace before meat and no swearing; but your right is based on the grounds that it is your house and that that is your way, and not because your way is best—though, to be sure, it may be.

Your own children may well expect you to know what you want

and what you believe in, and they will be helped by your faith, and will to a greater or less extent base their own standards on yours. But at the same time, and this is the point, do you not agree with me that the children themselves have their own beliefs and ideals, and of their own accord they seek order? Children do not like perpetual muddle or perpetual selfishness. Can you see that it must harm a child if you are so concerned with the establishment of your own rights in your own house that you fail to see and allow for the innate tendency of your infant and child to create a little world around himself that is his own affair and that has its own moral code? *If you are sufficiently confident about yourself* I think you will like to see how far you can let each of your children dominate the scene by his own impulses and schemes and ideas in a localised way, inside your wider influence. 'To-day it's my birthday and so everything's my accord', the little girl said, and this did not lead to chaos; it led to a day arranged not much unlike any other day, except that it was created by the child instead of by the mother, or nurse or schoolmistress.

Of course, this is the sort of thing a mother ordinarily does at the beginning of the infant's life. Not being able to be entirely at the beck and call of her infant, she gives the breast at regular intervals, which is the next best thing, and she often succeeds in giving the baby a short period of illusion in which he does not have to recognise yet that a dream breast does not satisfy, however lovely the dream. He cannot get fat on a dream breast. That is to say, to be good the breast must also belong to mother, who is external to him and independent of him. It is not enough for baby to have the idea that he would like a feed; it is also necessary for mother to have the idea that she would like to feed him. To recognise this is a hard task for a child, and a mother can protect her infant from too early or too abrupt disillusionment.

At first, too, the baby is felt to be important. If he needs food or cries from discomfort, everything goes by the board until his needs have been attended to; and he is allowed as far as possible to be impulsive—for instance, making messes for no better reason than that he wants to. It seems a curious change from the infant's point of view, when mother becomes strict, sometimes suddenly becomes strict because she has been frightened by the neighbours, and starts what is called 'training', never relaxing till she has made her infant conform to her standard of cleanliness. She thinks she has done very well if her baby gives up all hope of retaining his valuable spontaneity and valuable impulsiveness. As a matter of fact, too early and strict training in cleanliness often defeats its own ends, and a child clean at six months becomes defiantly or unconsciously dirty and exceedingly difficult to retrain. Fortunately, in many cases the child finds a way out and hope is not entirely lost, and the spontaneity merely hides in a symptom such as bed-wetting. (As one watching, and not having to wash and dry the sheets, I have been delighted before now to find the child of a rather domineering mother bed-wetting, sticking to his guns, though not exactly knowing what he is doing.) The reward is great for the mother who, while retaining her own values, can afford to wait for the child's own sense of values to develop. As a matter of fact, the trouble is not so much that the child has no sense of values, as that, at the start, people expect much more rigid standards of children than of adults. As an example I will mention the matter of saying 'thank you'. It is very likely that when your child is given a new bonnet by his aunt when he wanted a golliwog he will refuse to say even 'ta'. But you are trying to teach him to say 'ta' whether he feels grateful or not. Some children are conscientious objectors in this matter of saying 'thank you' when they do not mean it. So do not forget or despise the innate morality of your children. Perhaps we sometimes miss the significance of the fact that one of the earliest games is building, in spite of the fact that little children are so near to the great pleasure that belongs to impulsive destruction.

If you let each child develop his own right to dominate, you will be helping him. There will be the clash between your right to dominate and his, but this is natural and it is much better than imposing yourself on your child on the ground that you know best. You have a better reason—that you like your own way too. Let your child have a corner of the room or a cupboard or a bit of wall which is his or hers to mess or to tidy or to decorate, according to the child's mood, fancy, and whim. Each child of yours has a right to a bit of your house that he can call his own, and he also has a right to a bit of your time each day (and a bit of daddy's) on which he can count, and during which you are in his world. Of course the other extreme is not much use, when a mother, having no strong personal way of life herself, lets her child have all his own way. Sometimes you do see this, and then no one, not even the child, is happy.

3

Young Children and Other People

[1949]

THE emotional development of an infant starts at the beginning of his life. If we are to judge the way in which a human being deals with his fellow creatures, and see how he builds up his personality and life, we cannot afford to leave out what happens in the earliest years, months, and even weeks and days of his life. When we approach the problems of adults, for instance those associated with marriage, we are, of course, confronted with a great deal that belongs to later development. Nevertheless, in the study of any one individual we find the past as well as the present, the infant as well as the adult. Feelings and thoughts which can conveniently be called sexual appear at an early age, much earlier than was allowed for in the philosophy of our grandparents, and in a sense the whole range of human relationships is there from the start.

Let us see what happens when healthy small children play at fathers and mothers. On the one hand we can be sure that sex comes into the game, although very often not by direct representation. It is possible to detect many symbols of adult sex behaviour, but it is not with this that I am concerned at the present moment. More important from our point of view is that these children are enjoying in their play something which is based on their ability to feel identified with their parents. Obviously they have observed a great deal. One can see in their games that they are building a home, arranging the house, taking joint responsibility for the children, even maintaining a framework in which the children in this game can discover their own spontaneity. (For children become frightened of their own impulses if left entirely on their own.) We know this is healthy; if children can play together like this they will not need later on to be taught how to build a home. They know the essentials already. Putting it the other way round, is it possible to teach people how to build a home if they have never had it in them to play fathers and mothers? I should think probably not.

While we are glad to see children thus able to enjoy games which show their ability to become identified with the home and with the parents, and with a mature outlook and a sense of responsibility, these are not things that we want our children to achieve all day long. Indeed, it would be alarming if they did so. We expect the same children who play this game in the afternoon to be just greedy children at tea-time, jealous of each other at bedtime, naughty and defiant the next morning; for they are still children. If they are lucky their real home exists. In the setting of their real home, they can go on discovering their own spontaneity and individuality, letting themselves go, as a story-teller does, surprising himself at the ideas that turn up as he warms to his task. In real life they can use their own real parents, although in the game they seek in turns to be the parents themselves. We welcome the appearance of this game of home-building along with all the other games of teachers and pupils, doctors, nurses, and patients, bus drivers and passengers.

We can see the health in it all. But by the time children have reached this stage at which they play games, we can easily understand that they have already been through many complex processes of development, and these processes are, of course, not ever actually completed. If children need an ordinary good home with which to become identified, they also deeply need a stable home and a stable emotional environment in which they can have the opportunity to make steady and natural progress, in their own time, through the very early stages of development. By the way, it is not necessary for parents to know all that goes on in the minds of their small children, any more than they need know all about anatomy and physiology in order to give their children physical health. It is essential for them, however, to have the imagination to recognise that parental love is not merely a natural instinct within themselves, but it is something which a child absolutely needs of them.

The baby is in a bad way who is cared for by a mother who is well-meaning indeed, but who believes that babies are little more at the beginning than a bundle of physiology and anatomy and conditioned reflexes. No doubt he will be well fed, and he may achieve physical health and growth, but unless his mother can see the human being in the new-born infant, there is but little chance that mental health will be soundly based in such a way that the child in later life can have a rich stable personality that can not only adapt to the world, but also be part of the world which demands adaptation.

The trouble is that the mother naturally tends to be afraid of her great responsibility, and she easily flies to the textbooks and the rules and regulations. The proper care of an infant can only be done from the heart; perhaps I should say that the head cannot do it alone, can do it only if feelings are free.

Giving food is only one of the ways in which a mother makes herself known to her infant, but it is an important one, and some of the things that happen can best be described in terms of feeding. A mother could claim at the end of a successful breast-feeding experience that on a thousand occasions she placed her breast within reach of her baby, just at the time when the baby wanted something. In this way, she has given the infant reason to believe the world is a place in which there is hope of finding something like what is expected and imagined and needed. Gradually the infant has come to have a relationship to external objects. One can be reminded here of the philosophical problem: 'Is that object over there really there, or is it only imagined?' The relationship between subjective and objective reality can be discussed for hours. The child who has been sensitively fed at the beginning and sensitively managed in other ways has really got beyond any answer that can be given to this philosophical conundrum; whether the object is real or illusory has become relatively unimportant to him because he has found a mother who has been willing *to provide him with the illusion,* and to provide it unfailingly and for a long enough period so that the gulf that there can be between what can be imagined and what is actually to be found has been reduced for this child personally as much as it is possible to be reduced.

Such a child has established at the end of his nine or so months a good relationship to something outside himself which he is coming to recognise as his mother, a relationship which is able to survive all possible frustrations and complications and even loss by separation. The baby who has been fed mechanically and insensitively and with no one wanting actively to adapt to the needs of that particular infant is at a great disadvantage, and if such a baby can conceive of a devoted mother at all such a mother must remain an imaginary idealised figure.

We may easily find a mother who is unable to live in the world of the infant. Her child must live in her own world. Such a child may make very good progress from the point of view of the superficial observer. It may not be until adolescence or even later that he at last makes appropriate protest, and either breaks down or finds mental health only in defiance.

In contrast, the mother who actively adapts in a rich way gives her baby a basis for making contact with the world, and more than that, gives a richness to the baby's relationship with the world which can develop and come to fruition as maturity follows in the course of time. A not unimportant part of this initial relationship of the baby with the mother is the inclusion in it of powerful instinctual drives; the survival of the baby and the mother teaches the baby through experience that instinctual experiences and excited ideas can be allowed, and that they do not necessarily destroy the quiet type of relationship, friendship, and sharing.

It should not be concluded that every baby who is sensitively fed and managed by a devoted mother is necessarily bound to develop complete mental health. Even when the early experiences are good, everything gained has to be consolidated in the course of time. Nor should it be concluded that every baby who is brought up in an institution, or by a mother who is unimaginative or too frightened to trust her own judgment, is destined for the mental hospital or Borstal. Things are not so simple as this. I have deliberately simplified the problem for the sake of clarity.

Now let us see something of what the baby is like when he is born into good conditions. What is the healthy little child like, whose mother has treated him as a person in his own right from the start? Is he just nice, and good, and compliant? The answer is no, the normal child has a personal view of life from the beginning. Healthy babies often have quite strong feeding difficulties; they may be defiant and wilful in regard to their excretions; they protest often and vehemently with screaming, they kick their mothers and pull their mothers' hair, and they try to gouge their eyes out; in fact they are a nuisance. But they display spontaneous and absolutely genuine affectionate impulses, a hug here and a little bit of generosity there; through these things the mothers of such infants find reward.

Somehow the textbooks seem to like good, compliant, clean children, but these virtues are only of value when the children develop them in the course of time, because of their growing ability to become identified with the parental side of home life. This is rather like the natural progression in a child's artistic efforts. At first a child scribbles. Then comes a time when there is a relation between the marks and colours, and of the whole drawing to the size of the page. Now form as well as matter counts. This is so much more important than form that is taught in the old-fashioned art class.

Nowadays we so often speak of the maladjusted child, but the maladjusted child is one to whom the *world* has failed to adjust adequately at the beginning and in the early stages. The compliance of an infant is a terrible thing. It means that the parents are buying convenience at a heavy price, which will have to be paid over and over again either by them, or by society if the parents cannot stand the racket.

I should like to mention a difficulty in this matter of the earliest relationship between the mother and the infant which concerns any prospective mother. At the time of the birth of the baby and for the few days afterwards, the doctor must be an important person for her, the one who is responsible for what goes on, and in whom she has confidence. There is nothing more important at such a time than for the mother to know her doctor, and the nurse who works with the doctor. Unfortunately it cannot be assumed that the doctor who is so very skilled in regard to physical health and physical disease and with the whole problem of the management of child-birth is equally well informed in regard to the emotional tie between the baby and the mother. There is so much for a doctor to learn that he can hardly be expected to be an expert on the physical side and also to be right up to date with the latest that there is to be known about the psychology of mothers and their babies. It is always possible, therefore, that an excellent doctor or nurse may interfere, without meaning to do any harm at all, in this delicate matter of the first contact between mother and baby.

The mother indeed does need the doctor and the nurse, and their skill, and the framework which they provide enables her to put her worries aside. Within that framework, however, she needs to be able to find her infant and to enable her infant to find her. She needs to be able to let this happen in a natural way, not according to any rules that can be found in books.

Obviously this is a big subject, and it is very complex indeed when one comes to try to state both the mother's need for medical skill and at the same time her need to be left alone with her infant. However, it is worth mentioning that this difficulty can exist, and, in fact, mothers need not feel ashamed to find they are specialists just at this point where the doctor and the nurse are only in a position to assist.

There can be observed a general cultural tendency away from direct contact, away from the clinical, away from what used to be called vulgar, that is to say naked, natural, and real, and there is a tendency towards whatever is at one remove from actual physical contact and interchange. If it is so much more important to be an official on the Milk Marketing Board than to be milking a cow, one must expect the mother's first task to be despised.

There is another way in which the infant's emotional life lays the basis for the emotional life of the individual at a later stage. I have spoken about the way in which instinctual drives enter the relationship of the infant to the mother right from the beginning. Along with these powerful instincts are the aggressive elements, and also there is all the hate and anger that arise from frustration. The aggressive element in, and associated with, the excited love impulses makes life feel very dangerous, and because of this most individuals become to some extent inhibited. It is perhaps profitable to look at this part of the problem a little more closely.

I would say that the most primitive and early impulses are felt ruthlessly. If there is a destructive element in the early feeding impulse the infant is at first not concerned with the consequences. I am, of course, talking about the ideas, and not just about the actual physical processes which we can watch with our eyes. At first the infant is carried away by impulses, and only very gradually there comes the realisation that the thing attacked in an excited feeding experience is a vulnerable part of the mother, the other human being who is so much valued as a person in the quiet intervals between excitements and orgies. The excited infant violently attacks the mother's body in fantasy although the attack that we see is but feeble; satisfaction comes with the feeding experience, and for the time being the attack ceases. Every physical process is enriched by fantasy, which steadily develops definiteness and complexity as the baby grows. In the baby's fantasy the mother's body was torn open so that the good things could be got at and incorporated. How important it is, therefore, for a baby to have his mother consistently looking after him, looking after him over a period of time, surviving his attacks, and eventually there to be the object of the tender feeling and the guilt feeling and sense of concern for her welfare which come along in the course of time. Her continuing to be a live person in the baby's life makes it possible for the baby to find that innate sense of guilt which is the only valuable guilt feeling, and which is the main source of the urge to mend and to re-create and to give. There is a natural sequence of ruthless love, aggressive attack, guilt feeling, sense of concern, sadness, desire to mend and build and give; this sequence is the essential experience of infancy and early childhood and yet it cannot become a real thing unless the mother, or someone doing her job for her, is able to live through the phases with the infant, and so to make possible the integration of the various elements.

And here is yet another way of stating some of the things that the ordinary good mother is doing for her infant. Without undue difficulty and without knowing what she is doing, the average good parent is all the time helping the child to distinguish between the actual happenings and what goes on in the imagination. She is sorting out for the infant the actual from the enriching fantasy. We say she is being objective. In the matter of aggression this is particularly important. A mother protects herself from being bitten badly and she prevents the two-year-old child from hitting the new baby on the head with a poker, but at the same time she recognises the tremendous force and reality of the destructive and aggressive *ideas* that belong to the child who is behaving tolerably well, and she is not alarmed by ideas. She knows that ideas must be there, and when they gradually appear in play or in dreams she is not surprised, and she even provides stories and story-books which carry on the themes that arise spontaneously in the child mind. She does not try to prevent the child from having ideas of destruction, and in that way she enables innate guilt to develop in its own way. It is innate guilt that we hope will turn up as the infant develops, and for which we are willing to wait; imposed morality bores us.

The period in which one is called on to be a mother or father is certainly a time of self-sacrifice. The ordinary good mother knows without being told that during this time nothing must interfere with the continuity of the relationship between the child and herself. Does she know that when she is acting quite naturally in this way, not only is she laying the foundation of the mental health of her child, but also the child cannot achieve mental health without having at the beginning just that experience which she is taking so much trouble to provide?

4

What Do We Mean by a Normal Child?

[1946]

We often talk about difficult children, and we try to describe and classify their difficulties; we also talk of normality, or health, but it is much harder to describe a normal child. We know well enough what we mean by normal when we are speaking of the body. We mean that the child's development is somewhere about average considering the child's age, and that there is no physical disease. We know, too, what we mean by a normal intellect. But a child with a healthy body, and a normal or even supra-normal intellect, can still be very far from normal as a whole personality.

We could think in terms of behaviour, comparing a child with other children of the same age, but we would hesitate before labelling children abnormal because of their behaviour, since there are such wide variations in the normal and, indeed, in what is expected; a child cries when hungry, and the question is, what is the age of the child? It is not abnormal to cry when hungry at a year old. A child takes a penny out of his mother's bag. Again, at what age? Most children of two would do this sometimes. Or, watch two children who each act as if expecting to be hit; in one case there is no reality basis for the fear, whereas in the other, the child is always being hit at home. Or, a child is still feeding from the breast at three years old; this is very unusual in England, but in some parts of the world this is the custom. Not by comparing the behaviour of one child with another do we come to an understanding of what we mean by normal.

What we want to know is whether a child's personality is building up normally, and whether character is strengthening in a healthy way. Cleverness in a child will not make up for a hold-up in the maturing of the personality. If emotional development has got hung up at some spot, a child has to be going back whenever certain circumstances recur, to act as if still an infant or a little child. For instance, we say that someone is acting like a child if, whenever frustrated, that person changes into a nasty person, or has a heart attack. A so-called normal person has other ways of dealing with frustration.

I will try to say something positive about normal development. But first let us agree that the needs and feelings of infants are tremendously powerful. It is essential to look at the child as a human being who starts off with all the intense feelings of human beings, though his relation to the world is only beginning. People adopt all sorts of devices to try to recapture the feelings that belong to their own infancies and early childhood, feelings that are valuable because so intense.

On this assumption we may think of early childhood as a gradual process of the building up of belief. Belief in people and things is built up little by little through innumerable good experiences. 'Good' here means satisfactory enough, so that the need or the impulse can be said to have been met and justified. These good experiences are weighed against the bad experiences, 'bad' being the word we use when anger and hate and doubt turn up, as they inevitably do. Every human being has to find a place to operate from, and to build up there, in the self, an organisation of the instinctive urges; every human being has to develop a personal method of living with these impulses in the particular kind of world which has been allotted, and it is not easy. In fact, the main thing to point out to people about infants and children is that even if it has all sorts of good things about it, life for infants and children is not easy, and there is no such thing as life without tears, except where there is compliance without spontaneity.

From this fact—that life is inherently difficult and that no infant or child can avoid showing evidence of its difficulties—it follows that in every one there will be symptoms, any one of which, under certain conditions, could be a symptom of illness. Even the most kindly, understanding background of home-life cannot alter the fact that ordinary human development is hard, and indeed a perfectly adaptive home would be difficult to endure, because there would be no relief through justified anger.

So we are driven to the idea that there are two meanings to the word normal. One is useful to the psychologist, who needs a standard, and who has to call everything abnormal that is imperfect. The other is useful to doctors, parents, and teachers when they want to describe a child who seems likely eventually to grow up into a satisfactory member of society, and this in spite of the fact that symptoms and inconvenient behaviour problems are clearly present.

For instance, I know a baby boy who was born prematurely. Doctors would say this was abnormal. He would not feed for ten days, so his mother had to express milk and give it in a bottle. This is normal for a premature child and abnormal for a full-term child. From the day when he ought to have been born he took the breast, although slowly, only at his own rate. From the beginning he made tremendous demands on his mother, who found she could succeed only by following him, letting him decide when to start and when to leave off. Throughout infancy he screamed at every new thing, and the only way to get him to use a new cup, or a new bath, or a cot, was to introduce him to it, and then to wait and wait till he turned to it. The degree to which he needed his own way spelt abnormality to a psychologist, but, because he had this mother who was willing to follow him, we can still call this child normal. As a further evidence of finding life difficult the child developed very intense screaming attacks, in which he got beyond being consoled, so that the only thing to do was to leave him in his cot and wait nearby till he recovered. In the attacks he did not know his mother, so she could not be of any use to him until he started to recover, when she became once more a mother he could use. The child was sent to a psychologist for special investigation, but while the mother was waiting for an appointment she found that the child and she together were becoming able to understand each other without help. The psychologist left them to it. He could see abnormality in the child and in the mother, but he preferred to call them normal, and to let them have the valuable experience of recovering from a difficult situation by means of their own natural resources.

For my own part, I use the following description of a normal child. A normal child *can* employ any or all of the devices nature has provided in defence against anxiety and intolerable conflict. The devices employed (in health) are related to the kind of help that is available. Abnormality shows in a *limitation* and a *rigidity* in the child's capacity to employ symptoms, and a relative lack of relationship between the symptoms and what can be expected in the way of help. Naturally, one has to allow for the fact that in earliest infancy there is but little capacity for judging what type of help is available, and a corresponding need for close adaptation on the part of the mother.

Take bed-wetting, a common enough symptom which almost every one has to deal with who has to deal with children. If by bed-wetting a child is making effective protest against strict management, sticking up for the rights of the individual, so to speak, then the symptom is not an illness; rather it is a sign that the child still hopes to keep the individuality which has been in some way threatened. In the vast majority of cases, bed-wetting is doing its job, and given time, and with ordinary good management, the child will become able to leave off the symptom and adopt other methods of asserting the self.

Or take refusal of food—another common symptom. It is absolutely normal for a child to refuse food. I assume that the food you offer is good. The point really is that a child cannot always *feel* the food to be good. A child cannot *always* feel that good food is deserved. Given time and calm management the child will eventually find out what to call good, and what to call bad; in other words, will develop likes and dislikes, like the rest of us.

It is these devices that are normally employed by our children that we call symptoms, and we say that a normal child is able to have any kind of symptom in appropriate circumstances. But with an ill child it is not the symptoms that are the trouble; it is the fact that the symptoms are not doing their job, and are as much a nuisance to the child as to the mother.

So although bed-wetting, and refusal of food, and all sorts of other symptoms can be serious indications for treatment, they need not be so. In fact, children who can surely be called normal can be shown to have such symptoms, and to have them simply because life is difficult, inherently difficult for every human being, for every one from the very beginning.

From what do the difficulties arise? *Firstly,* there is the fundamental clash between the two kinds of reality, that of the external world which can be shared by every one, and that of each child's personal inner world of feelings, ideas, imagination. From birth each baby is constantly being introduced to the fact of the external world. In the early feeding experiences, ideas are compared with fact; that which is wanted, expected, thought up, is weighed against what is supplied, against what is dependent for its existence on the will and wish of another person. Throughout life there must always be distress in connection with this essential dilemma. Even the best external reality is disappointing because it is not also imaginary, and although perhaps to some extent it can be manipulated, it is not under magical control. One of the chief tasks before those who care for a little child is to give help in the painful transition from illusion to disillusion, by simplifying as far as possible the problem immediately in front of a child at any one moment. Much of the screaming and the temper tantrums of infancy range round this tug-of-war between inner and outer reality, and the tug-of-war must be reckoned normal.

A special part of this particular process of disillusionment is the child's discovery of the joy of the immediate impulse. If the child is to grow up, however, to join with the others of a group, a great deal of the joy that belongs to spontaneity has to be given up. Yet, nothing can be given up that has not first been found and possessed. How difficult it is for the mother to make sure that each infant in turn gets the feeling of having had the essentials of love, before being asked to do with less than all! Clashes and protests are indeed to be expected normally in connection with such painful learning.

Then, *secondly,* there is the awful discovery the infant begins to make that with excitement there go very destructive thoughts. When feeding, a child is liable to feel the urge to destroy everything that is good, the food, and the person who has the food to give him. This is very frightening, or gradually becomes so as the infant recognises a person behind the child care, or because the child comes to be very fond of the person who at feed-times is there as if exactly to be destroyed or used up. And, along with this, there comes a feeling that there will be nothing left if everything has been destroyed; and what happens then, should hunger return?

So what is to be done? Sometimes the child will just stop being eager about food, thereby gaining peace of mind but losing something valuable, because if there is no eagerness there cannot be the experience of full satisfaction. So here we have a symptom—inhibition of healthy greediness—which we must expect to some extent in children whom we shall call normal. If, in trying all sorts of dodges to get round the symptom, the mother knows what all the fuss is about, she will not be so liable to get in a panic and will be able to play for time, always a good thing in child care. It is wonderful what the human infant and child can manage in the end, if someone who is personally responsible is calmly and consistently continuing to act naturally.

All this only concerns the relation between the infant and the mother. Only too soon, added to other troubles, are those that belong to the child's recognition that there is also father to be reckoned with. A lot of the symptoms you note in your child have to do with the complications that arise naturally out of this fact and the wider implications. Yet we would not want there to be no father on this account. It is obviously better that all sorts of symptoms should appear as a direct result of a child's jealousy of the father, or love of him, or because of mixed feelings, than that the child should go straight ahead without having had to cope with this further hard fact of external reality.

And the arrival of new children causes upsets which likewise are desirable rather than deplorable.

And *lastly,* for I cannot mention everything, the child soon begins to create a personal inner world in which battles are lost and won, a world in which magic holds sway. From children's pictures and play you will see something of this inner world, which must be taken seriously. As this inner world feels to the child to have a position, feels to be located in the body, you must expect the child's body to be involved. For instance, all sorts of body pains and bodily upsets will accompany the strains and stresses in the inner world. And in an attempt to control inner phenomena a child will have aches and pains, or will make magic gestures, or dance round like one possessed, and I do not want you to think, when you have to deal with these 'mad' things in your own child, that the child is ill. You must expect a child to become possessed by all kinds of real and imaginary people, and by animals and things, and sometimes these imaginary people and animals will come outside, so that you will have to pretend you see them too, unless you want to cause great confusion through expecting your child to be grown-up while still a child. And do not be surprised if you have to cater for imaginary playmates who are entirely real to your child, derived from the inner world, yet for the time being kept external to the personality for some good reason.

Instead of going on trying to explain why life is normally difficult I will end with a friendly hint. Put a lot of store on a child's ability to play. If a child is playing there is room for a symptom or two, and if a child is able to enjoy play, both alone and with other children, there is no very serious trouble afoot. If in this play is employed a rich imagination, and if also pleasure is got from games that depend on exact perception of external reality, then you can be fairly happy, even if the child in question is wetting the bed, stammering, displaying temper tantrums, or repeatedly suffering from bilious attacks or depression. The playing shows that this child is capable, given reasonably good and stable surroundings, of developing a personal way of life, and eventually of becoming a whole human being, wanted as such, and welcomed by the world at large.

5

The Only Child

[1945]

I AM going to discuss children who, although they live in ordinary good homes, have no brothers and sisters; only children. The question is: in what ways does it really matter whether a child is an only child or one of a family?

Now, when I look round and see so many only children I realise that there must be very good reasons for having only one. Of course, in many cases parents would do anything to have a large family, but some reason or other has cropped up which makes this impossible. But often there is a conscious plan to have no more than one child. I suppose the common reason given, if one asks why two married people intend to have only one child, is that it is a question of economics. 'We simply cannot afford more than one child'.

Babies undoubtedly are an expense. I think it would be most unwise to advise parents to ignore their inner promptings with regard to the financial side of family life. We all know of legitimate and illegitimate babies scattered all over the place by men and women with too little of that sense of responsibility which makes young people naturally hesitate before embarking on large families. If people like to speak in terms of money, let them, but really I think that what they doubt is whether they are able to support a large family without losing too much personal freedom. If two children do really make twice as much demand on mother and father as one child makes, then it is as well that the cost is counted in advance. Only one might doubt whether several children are, in fact, so much more of a burden than an only child can be.

Forgive me for calling a child a burden. Children *are* a burden, and if they bring joy it is because they are wanted, and two people have decided to take that kind of a burden; in fact, have agreed to call it not a burden, but a baby. There is a significant humorous saying: 'May all your troubles be little ones!' If we talk sentimentally about children people will give up having them altogether; mothers can enjoy washing and mending, but do not let us forget the work and the unselfishness it all means.

There are some undoubted advantages that a child can get out of being an only child. I think that the fact that the parents are able to devote themselves to the one baby means that it is possible for them to make better arrangements than they could otherwise do for that baby to have an uncomplicated infancy. That is to say, the baby can start with the simplest possible relationship between child and mother, and this bit of the world gradually develops complexity not faster than the developing infant can allow for. This foundation of existence in a simplified environment can give a sense of stability which can be a great stand-by for the whole of life. Also, of course, I should mention other important things, such as the food, clothing, and education which parents can easily give to their only child.

Now let me turn to some of the disadvantages. The obvious disadvantage of being an only child is the lack of playmates, and the lack of that richness of experience which can result from a child's various relationships to older and younger brothers and sisters. There is so much in the play of children which grown-ups cannot get into touch with; even if they understand it, they cannot enter into it for such long periods as the child would like. In fact, if grown-ups play with a child the natural madness in the child's play becomes too evident. So, if there are no other children, a child becomes stunted in play and misses the pleasures that belong to inconsequence, irresponsibility, and impulsiveness; the tendency is for the only child to become precocious, and to prefer listening and talking in grown-up company and helping mother about the house, or using father's tools. It becomes silly to play. Children who play together have an infinite capacity for inventing play-details, and they also go on playing for long periods without tiring.

But I think there is something even more important; it is valuable for a child to experience the entry of a new brother or sister into the family. In fact, I cannot over-emphasise the value of this experience. There is something quite fundamental in the fact of pregnancy, and a child has missed a great deal who has missed seeing the changes in his mother, finding himself unable to be comfortable on her lap, gradually coming to the reason for this, and getting tangible proof of what he secretly knows all the time in the eventual appearance of the new baby, and the simultaneous return of mother to normal. Even if there are many children who find this rather strong meat, and who fail to cope with the tremendous feelings and conflicts aroused, nevertheless it remains true, I think, that every child who has missed such an experience, and who has never seen mother giving milk from her breasts, and bathing and caring for an infant, is less rich than the child who has witnessed these things. And perhaps little children wish to have babies as much as grown-ups do. But they cannot, and dolls only partly satisfy them. By proxy they can have children if their mother has them.

One thing the only child especially lacks is the experience of finding hate turn up; the child's own hate, as the new baby threatens what seemed to be a settled and safe relation to the mother and father. It is so usual as to be called normal when a child is upset at the birth of a new one. The child's first comment is not usually polite: 'It's got a face like a tomato'; in fact parents should feel relieved when they hear the direct expression of conscious dislike, and even violent hate, at the birth of a new child. This hate will gradually give way to love as the new infant develops into a human being, who can be played with, and of whom one can be proud. The first reaction, however, can be of fear and hate, and the impulse may be to put the new baby in the dustbin. I think that it is a very valuable experience for a child to find that the younger brother or sister for whom love is beginning to develop is the same as the new baby who was hated a few weeks ago and actually wished away. For all children a big difficulty is the legitimate expression of hate, and the only child's relative lack of opportunity for expressing the aggressive side of his nature is a serious thing. Children who grow up together play games of all kinds, and so have a chance to come to terms with their own aggressiveness, and they have valuable opportunities for discovering on their own that they do mind when they really hurt someone they love.

Another thing, the arrival of new babies means that father and mother are still fond of each other. I personally think that children get valuable reassurance about the relations between father and mother through the advent of new babies; and it is always vitally important to children that they should be able to feel that mother and father are sexually drawn together, maintaining the structure of family life.

A family of children has one other advantage over an only child. In a big family there is a chance for children to play all sorts of different roles in relation to each other, and all this prepares them for life in larger groups and eventually in the world. Only children as they grow older, especially if they have not many cousins, find it difficult to meet other boys and girls on a casual basis. Only children are all the time looking for *stable* relationships and this tends to scare off the casual acquaintance, whereas the members of large families are used to meeting the friends of their brothers and sisters, and they have a good deal of practical experience of human relationships by the time they reach the age of walking-out.

Parents can certainly do a very great deal for an only child, and many prefer to do their best in this way, but they do also stand to suffer. In war-time especially they have to be very brave to let their child go and fight, although it may be the only good thing from the child's point of view. Boys and girls need the freedom to run risks, and it is a serious frustration to them if they cannot do so because, being only children, they may hurt their parents too much if they themselves get hurt. There is also the fact that a man and woman are enriched by every child they nurture and launch into the world.

Furthermore, there is the matter of the care of father and mother as the child grows older. When there are several children the care of father and mother can be shared. Clearly, only children can be weighed down by their own wish to look after their parents. Perhaps parents ought to think of this in advance. They sometimes forget that when they looked after the child, the child quickly grew up and was young only for a few years. But the child may be looking after the parents (and may want to do so) for twenty or thirty years, or more; always an indefinite period. If there are several children it is much easier for the care of ageing parents to remain a pleasure to the end. As a matter of fact, it does sometimes happen that young married people who would like to have several children are unable to do so because they have the great responsibility of their ageing or ill parents who did not have enough children to enable this work to be shared, and so enjoyed.

You will notice that I have discussed the advantages and disadvantages of being an only child on the assumption that the child is an ordinary healthy, normal individual, with an ordinary good home. Obviously a great deal more could be said if one were to think of abnormalities. For instance, parents who have a backward child have a special problem which deserves special consideration, and many children are so difficult to manage that parents naturally wonder whether other children would be harmed by the one difficult child, and the type of management which this child forces them to adopt. And then there is the equally important case of the child whose parents are in some way or other ill—either physically or psychologically. For instance, some mothers and fathers are more or less always depressed, or they worry; some are so frightened of the world that they build their home on the basis that the world is hostile to it. An only child has to discover this and deal with it all alone. As a friend said to me, 'For me there was an odd feeling of closed-in-ness; perhaps too much love, too much attention, too much possessiveness made one feel shut up with these parents who imagined, long after it had ceased to be true, that they were the whole of one's world. For me this was infinitely the worst part of being an only child. My parents were outwardly wise about the matter. They sent me to school when I could hardly walk, and let me practically live with the children next door, but at home there was this odd drawing-in as though family ties were infinitely more important than others. If there is no one in the family who is one's contemporary, all this is apt to fill a child with a kind of pride.'

You will have gathered that in my personal opinion there are more arguments in favour of the large family than in favour of the only child. However, it is much better to have one or two children, and to do one's best for the few, than to have an unlimited number without the physical strength and the emotional stamina to cope with them. If there must be one child in a family and no more, let it be remembered that other people's children can be invited to the house, and that this can start early. And the fact that two little children bang each other on the head does not mean they ought not to have met. When there are no children available there can be dogs and other pets, and there are nursery schools and kindergartens. If the immense disadvantages of onlyness are understood, they can be got round to some extent providing the will to get round them exists.

6

Twins

[1945]

The first thing to say about twins is that they are perfectly natural phenomena, and really nothing to be sentimental or facetious about. I know many mothers who have loved having twins, and I know many twins who have liked being twins. But nearly all mothers say they would not have actually chosen twins had they been asked, and twins, even those who seem quite contented with their lot, usually tell me they would have preferred to have come one at a time.

Twins have their own particular problems to solve. Whatever the advantages of being a twin, there are also disadvantages. If I can help, it will be not so much by telling you what to do as by giving you a hint or two of the main difficulty.

Before I go any further I must remind you that there are two different sorts of twins, because the problem is not exactly the same for each kind. You know that every baby develops from one minute cell, a fertilised ovum or egg cell. As soon as the ovum is fertilised it starts growing, and it divides into two. Each of these two cells divides into two, making four, and the four become eight, and this goes on till the new individual is made up of millions of cells of all types, all related to each other, and as much a unity as was the original fertilised ovum. Sometimes, after the first division of the newly-fertilised ovum, each of the two cells divides and then develops independently, and this is the beginning of the identical twins; two babies developing from the same fertilised ovum. Identical twins are always of the same sex, and they are usually very much like each other in appearance, at least at first.

The other kind of twins may or may not be of the same sex, as they are just like any other brothers and sisters, except that they developed from ova that happened to be fertilised at the same moment. The two ova in this case grow side by side in the womb. Twins of this kind do not necessarily look alike, any more than other brothers and sisters do.

Looking at twins of either kind we easily feel that it must be nice for each child to have company—never to be alone, especially as the two get older. There is a snag, however, and to understand this we have to remind ourselves of the way that infants develop. In ordinary circumstances, and with ordinary good management, infants start immediately after birth to form the basis of their personalities and of their individuality, and to discover their own importance. We all like unselfishness and a willingness to allow for the other person's point of view, and hope to find these virtues in our children, but, if we study the emotional development of the infant, we find that unselfishness only comes in a healthy and stable way if it is based on a primary experience of selfishness. It might be said that without this *primary selfishness* a child's unselfishness gets clogged up with resentment. Anyway, this primary selfishness is no more than the infant's experience of good mothering, a good mother being willing, at first, to fit in with her baby's desires as far as possible, letting the baby's impulses dominate the situation, and being contented to wait for the baby's ability to allow for the other person's point of view to develop in the course of time. At the start a mother must be able to give her baby the sense of possession, and the feeling that he has control over her, the feeling that she has been created for the occasion. Her own private life is not forced on the baby at first. With the experience of primary selfishness in his bones the baby will be able to become unselfish later without too much resentment.

Now, in the ordinary way, when babies come in ones, each little human being can take what time is needed to recognise the right of his mother to other interests, and it is well known that every child finds the arrival of a new child a complication, sometimes quite a serious one. No mother would worry if her baby failed to appreciate the benefits of the companionship of other babies till well after the first birthday, and even two-year-olds may bash each other rather than play together, at first. For indeed each baby has his own time for welcoming a brother or sister; and it is an important moment when a little child can genuinely 'allow' (that is, give) his mother a new pregnancy.

Now, the twin always has another baby to cope with, quite apart from the development of any willingness to allow an addition to the family.

This is one of the times when we see the fallacy of the view that little things do not matter in the early months, because it matters very much whether twins do, or do not, feel that they each had possession of mother at the start. The mother of twins has an extra task on top of everything else, which is to give the whole of herself to two babies at once. To some extent she must fail, and the mother of twins must be content to do her best, and hope that the children will eventually find advantages that will compensate for this inherent disadvantage of the twin state.

It is impossible for one mother to meet two infants' immediate needs at once. For instance, she cannot take up each of two children first, whether to feed them, or to change their napkins, or to bath them. She can try very hard to be fair, and it will repay her if she takes this matter seriously from the beginning, but it cannot be easy.

As a matter of fact she will find her aim is not to treat each child alike, but to treat each child as if that one were the only one. That is to say, she will be trying to find the differences between each infant from the moment of birth. She, of all people, must know each from the other easily, even if she has to tell one at first by a little mark on the skin, or by some other trick. She will usually come to find that the two temperaments are different, and that if she easily acts in relation to each as a total personality, each will develop personal characteristics. It is thought that a lot of the difficulty about twins arises out of the fact that they are not always recognised as different from each other, even where they are different, either because of the fun of it, or because there is no one who thinks this task worth the trouble. I know of a quite good home in which the matron never managed to learn to distinguish between two twin girls, although the other children had no difficulty in knowing one from the other; in fact the two girls really had quite distinct personalities. The matron used to call each one 'Twin'.

It is no solution to look after one yourself and to hand the other over to a nurse. You might have to share the care of the children with someone else for some good reason, if you are not in good health, for instance; but by that method you will not do more than postpone things, because one day the twin you handed over is going to be very jealous of the one you kept, even if the better mothering was done by the helper.

Mothers of twins seem to agree that even when the twins enjoy at times being mistaken for each other, these same children need their own mother to recognise the identity of each without trouble. It is essential in every case that there should be no confusion among the children themselves, and for that there must be some person in their lives who is quite clear about them. A mother I know had identical twins, exactly alike to outsiders, but distinguished easily by their mother from the beginning, because of their temperaments. In the first week or so this mother complicated her feeding routine by wearing a red shawl. One twin reacted to this, and simply gazed at the shawl—perhaps at its bright colour—and lost interest in the breast. The other, however, was unaffected by the shawl, and fed as usual. After this the mother felt not only that the two were two persons, but also that they had already ceased living parallel experiences. This particular mother got round the who-to-feed-first difficulty by having the feeds ready well on time, and feeding first the infant that seemed more eager. It was usually easy to decide by the crying. I do not say this method would suit all cases.

Certainly the main complication in the upbringing of twins is this question of the personal treatment and management of each, so that the wholeness and oneness of each gets full recognition. Even if there were twins that were exactly alike there would still be the need for their own mother to have a whole relation to each.

The mother I spoke about just now told me she found it a good idea to put one baby to sleep in the front garden, and the other in the back. Of course, you may not happen to have two gardens, but you may be able to arrange things somehow so that when one infant cries you will not always have to have the two crying. Not only is it a pity from your point of view to have the two at it at once, but also when crying a baby likes to dominate the scene; it is maddening to have a rival in early infancy at the stage of natural dictatorship, and I have known the effects of this sort of thing persist long into a twin's life.

I said that twins of one kind are called identical twins. Surely this word gives the whole show away. If the children *were* identical they would each be the same, they would add up to one, so to speak, which is absurd. They are similar, but not identical; the danger is that people will treat them as identical, and as I have said, if people do this the twins will themselves feel muddled about their own identities. And infants do become very muddled about their own identities apart from being twins; it is only gradually that they become sure of themselves. As you know, it is quite a while after words are used that children use pronouns. They say 'mum' and 'dad' and 'more' and 'dog' long before they say 'I' and 'you' and 'we'. It is quite possible for twins to sit in a pram, each thinking the other is not a separate person. Indeed, it would be more natural for an infant to think it to be himself at the other end of the pram (rather like looking in a mirror) than to say (in infant language) 'hullo, there's my twin opposite me'. But when one gets lifted out of the pram the other feels lost and cheated. Here is a difficulty that any baby may have, but that twins *must* have, and they can only hope to manage if we play our part, and know them as two people. Later, if the twins themselves become quite confident about their identities they may enjoy exploiting their likeness to each other, and then, and not before then, is the time for fun and games on the theme of mistaken identity.

Finally, do twins like each other? This is a question that twins must answer. From what I am told, I feel that the idea that twins are specially fond of each other needs looking into. Often they accept each other's company, enjoy playing together, and hate to be separated, and yet fail to convince one that they love each other. Then one day they discover that they hate each other like poison, and at last the possibility that they may get to love each other has come. This will not fit all cases, but where two children have had to put up with each other willy-nilly they cannot know whether they would have chosen to know each other. After the hate is expressed, the love has a chance. So you will not take it too much for granted that your twins want to spend their lives together, will you? They may, but they may not, and they may even be grateful to you, or to some chance thing like measles, for separating them, it being much easier to become a whole person alone than in company with one's twin.

7

Stealing and Telling Lies

[1949]

THE mother who has had several healthy children will know that each one of them presented acute problems every now and again, especially when 2 and 3 and 4 years old. One child had a period of night-screaming of very severe intensity so that the neighbours thought that she was being ill-treated. Another one absolutely refused to be trained to be clean. Another one was so clean and good that the mother was worried lest the child should be completely lacking in spontaneity and personal enterprise. Yet another of her children was liable to terrific temper tantrums, perhaps with head banging and the holding of breath until the mother was at her wit's end, and the child was blue in the face and as near to having a fit as possible. A long list could be made of this sort of thing happening naturally in the course of family life. One of these uncomfortable things that happen, and one that sometimes gives rise to special difficulties, is the habit of stealing.

Little children quite regularly take pennies out of their mothers' handbags. Usually there is no problem here whatever. The mother is quite tolerant of the way the child carries on, turning out the contents of her bag, and generally messing things up. She is rather amused, when she troubles to notice it. She may even have two bags, one of which the child never gets to at all, while another more workaday one is available for the little child's exploration. Gradually the child just grows out of this, and nothing more is thought of it. The mother quite rightly feels that this is healthy and a part of the child's initial relation to herself, and so to people in general.

We can easily see why it is, however, that occasionally one can find a mother really worried when her little child takes things that belong to her, and hides them. She has had experience of the other extreme, the thieving older child. There is nothing more disturbing to the happiness of a household than the presence in it of an older child (or grown-up for that matter) who is liable to steal. Instead of the general trusting of every one, and a free and easy way of leaving things all over the place, there has to be a specialised technique designed to protect important possessions such as money, chocolates, sugar, etc. In this case there is someone ill in the house. Many people get a very nasty feeling when they think of this. They feel ill at ease when they are confronted with thieving just as they do when the word masturbation is mentioned. Apart from their having met with thieves, people may find themselves very definitely upset at the very thought of thieving, because of battles they themselves have fought over their own thieving tendencies in their own childhood. It is because of this uncomfortable feeling about out-and-out thieving that mothers sometimes worry unnecessarily about the quite normal tendency of little children to take things from their own mothers' possessions.

After a moment's thought, it will be seen that in an ordinary household, one in which there is no ill person who could be called a thief, actually quite a lot of stealing goes on; only it is not called stealing. A child goes into the larder and takes a bun or two, or helps himself to a lump of sugar out of the cupboard. In a good home no one calls the child who does this a thief. (Yet the same child in an institution may be punished and branded because of the rules that happen to obtain there.) It may be necessary for parents to make rules in order to keep the home a going concern. They may have to make a rule that whereas the children can always go and take bread, or perhaps a certain kind of cake, they may not take special cakes, and may not eat sugar from the store-cupboard. There is always a certain amount of to-and-fro about these things, and life in a household to some extent consists in the working out of the relation between the parents and the children in these and similar terms.

It is not quite enough, however, to say to a mother that a normal little child is liable to steal from her, and that this means nothing at all except that he loves her, and then to go on and describe as ill the older child who has a compulsion to steal. The mother who is thinking things out wants to know what is the connection between these two phenomena. I shall try to find a way of stating this clearly. In any case there is a very indistinct border-line between the common and healthy stealing of the little child from his own mother and the thieving of the ill and older child. In most cases, when an older child is ill in this way, it can be found that the first theft was of pennies from mother's bag, or possibly of sugar from the cupboard.

Moreover, we have to learn to recognise a normal transition period in which the small child is growing into the slightly older one who begins to feel that it is wrong to steal things. This transition does not necessarily take place easily or suddenly. There can quite ordinarily be a period of difficulty, a time in which the little child is alternately horrified at the idea of stealing, and, in fact, stealing. This may show in the reaction to the birth of another child. A child of 4 may be very indignant when his baby brother or sister goes for the mother's bag, and may be found smacking the baby for what is really quite an innocent act; at the same time this four-year-old may be liable at times to steal secretly from mother.

It can easily be imagined what a tremendous guilt feeling can hang round this sort of situation. The four-year-old child who is like this is in the painful position of being split into two people, one who is more fiercely moral than the parents, and the other who is momentarily very wicked by his own standards. A child in this state automatically becomes a liar if suddenly accused. If the mother or father should take this boy aside and ask him about the theft, they will be talking to the super-moralist, and they will be in effect asking him to acknowledge that he is also a wicked thief. He will be unable to do this, and, in fact, if the investigation is pursued ruthlessly the child must become more seriously split in his personality. The lies he tells are his own attempt to explain to himself what he is (by the very nature of things) unable to explain. Parents who understand this will easily be able to deal gently with the occasional lapses of the child who is with some difficulty making a transition from the natural thieving of the early years to the later stage in which, if all goes well, his strict self and his impulsive self come to terms, so that he becomes able to manage his primitive love impulses without too severely disrupting his own moral sense. In any case, as the years pass, there will be new ways out. The parents will be allowing an absolutely regular and reliable weekly wage, the pocket money. This will deal in advance with the impulse to steal money. Also there will be birthdays, Christmas, and other reliable dates on which gifts can be confidently expected. Just before a gift day a child can allow his thieving self to come to life in the expectation of birthday presents, and to some extent he will find enough real gratification through the actual experiences, so that the primitive love impulses, which are greedy, ruthless, and magical, are for the time being satisfied without having had to be denied and lost to the child. Moreover, as the child gets older the body becomes more manageable. Excitements of one kind and another come under the control of the rest of the child's self. It becomes possible to do things deliberately. As confidence in the world increases, the child becomes able to wait; and sexual excitements become linked to ideas about people, and therefore become enriched by what these people themselves can contribute to the relationship in the way of positive values and understanding. By these and other means the ordinary child with an ordinary good home of his own passes into a social being, without serious antisocial incident.

8

Visiting Children in Hospital

[1951]

EVERY child has a line of life that starts at any rate from birth, and it is our job to see that it does not get broken. There is a continuous process of development within, which can make steady progress only if the care of the infant or small child is steady too. As soon as the infant as a person has begun to make relationships with people, these relationships are very intense and cannot be tampered with without danger. There is no need for me to labour this point since mothers naturally hate to let their children go away until the children are ready for the experience, and of course they are eager to go and see them if they have to be away from home.

At the present time there is a wave of enthusiasm for ward visiting. The trouble with waves of enthusiasm is that they may override real difficulties and sooner or later there comes a reaction. The only sensible thing is to get people to understand the reasons for and against visiting. And there are some really big difficulties from the nursing point of view.

If you were a Sister, I wonder why you would be doing this work? It may have started by being just one of the many ways of earning a living, but you soon found that you got caught up in nursing and that you got very keen, and you took tremendous trouble to learn all the very complicated techniques; and eventually you became a Sister. As a Sister you would work long hours, and that will always be true, because there will never be enough good Sisters, and it is difficult to share this work. Think what it is like to have absolute responsibility for twenty to thirty children who are not your own. Many of these children are very ill and require skilled handling. And you are responsible for all that is done for them, even for what the junior nurses do when you are not looking. You become terribly keen to get the children well, and this may mean following very definite lines laid down by the doctor. As well as all this, you have to be ready to deal with doctors and medical students, and these are human beings too.

When there is no visiting, the Sister takes the child into her care and the very best that is in her is roused. She would much rather be on duty than off duty very often, because she is always wondering what is happening in her ward. Some of the children get very dependent on her and cannot bear her to go off duty without saying good-bye. And they want to know exactly when she is coming back. The whole thing appeals to the best in human nature.

Now what happens when we have visiting? Immediately there is a difference, or at any rate there can be. From now on the responsibility for the child is never wholly with the Sister. This can work wonderfully well, and the Sister may be glad to share responsibility; but if she is very busy, and especially if there are some rather trying cases in the ward, and some rather trying mothers visiting it, it is much simpler to do the whole thing oneself than to share.

You would be surprised if I were to start to tell you things that happen during visiting. After the parents have gone the children are quite often sick, and what they bring up tells tales. Perhaps it does not matter much, this little episode of sickness after visiting, but it may reveal that the most unexpected children have been given carrots, and that the child on a diet has had sweets, which completely upsets the whole investigation on which his future treatment is to be based.

The fact is that in the visiting-hour the Sister has to let go of the control of the situation, and I think she sometimes really has no idea what goes on during that time. And there is no way round this. And, quite apart from food indiscretions, there is the menace of infection.

Another difficulty, as a very good Sister of a ward in a hospital has told me, is that since they have been allowed to visit daily, mothers think that their children are always crying in hospital, which of course is just not true. It is true that if you visit your child, your visits will often cause distress. You keep up the child's memory of you every time you go to the ward. You revive the wish to be home, so it must be that often you will leave the child crying. But this kind of distress, we think, is not nearly as harmful to the child as the distress that has gone over into indifference. If you have to leave the child so long that you are forgotten, the child will recover after a day or two and stop being distressed, and will adopt the nurses and the other children, and will develop a new life. In this case you have been forgotten and you will have to be remembered again afterwards.

It would not be so bad if the mothers were contented to go in and see their children for a few minutes and then go out again; but mothers do not feel like this, naturally. As will be expected, they go into the ward and use the whole time that is allowed. Some seem to be almost 'making love' to their child; they bring presents of all kinds, and especially food, and they demand affectionate response; and then they take quite a long time going, standing waving at the door till the child is absolutely exhausted by the effort of saying good-bye. And the mothers are quite liable to go to the Sister on the way out, and say something about the child's not being warmly enough clad or not having enough to eat for dinner or something like that. Only a few mothers take the moment of leaving as the right opportunity to thank the Sister for what she is doing, which is really quite a big thing. It is very difficult to admit that someone is looking after your own child as well as you could yourself.

So you see that if the Sister were asked, just after the parents have gone: 'Sister, what would you do about visiting if you were a dictator?' she might very likely say, 'I would abolish it'. But still she may agree, at a more favourable moment, that visiting is a natural and a good thing. The doctors and nurses can see it is worth while to allow it if they can stand it, and if the parents can be asked to co-operate.

* * *

I was saying that we find that anything that breaks up the child's life into fragments is harmful. Mothers know this, and they welcome daily visiting which makes it possible for them to keep in touch with their children during those unfortunate times when there is a need for hospital care.

It seems to me that when children *feel* ill the whole problem is much easier; every one understands what to do. Words seem so useless when one is talking to a small child, and they are unnecessary when a child feels very ill. The child just feels that something will be arranged that will help, and if this involves a stay in hospital this is accepted, even if tearfully. But when a child has to be put into hospital at a time when there is no feeling of being unwell, it is altogether different. I remember a child who was playing in the street when suddenly the ambulance came up, and she was whisked away to a fever hospital, although she was feeling well, because the day before it had been discovered at the hospital (through a throat examination) that she was a diphtheria carrier. You can imagine how awful this was for the child, who could not even be allowed to go in and say good-bye to her family. When we cannot explain ourselves we must expect a certain amount of loss of faith; actually, the particular child I am thinking about never really recovered from the experience. Perhaps, if visiting had been allowed, the outcome would have been more happy. If for nothing else it seems to me that the parents should be able to visit such a child so as to be able to take his anger while it is at white heat.

I have spoken of a need for hospital care as being *unfortunate*, but it can work out the other way. When your child is old enough, a hospital experience, or a stay away from home with an aunt, may be very valuable, enabling the home to be looked at from outside. I remember a boy of 12 who said, after he had been away at a convalescent home for a month. 'You know, I don't think I really am my mother's darling. She always gives me everything I want, but she doesn't really love me, somehow'. He was quite right too; his mother was trying hard, but she had big difficulties of her own which got in the way in her dealings with her children, and it was quite healthy for this particular boy to be able to see his mother from a distance. He went back ready to tackle the home situation in a new way.

Because of their own difficulties some parents are not ideal. How does this affect hospital visiting? Well, if when parents visit they bicker in front of the child it is naturally a very painful thing at the time, and the child worries about it afterwards. Such a thing can seriously affect the child's return to bodily health. And some people just cannot keep promises; they say they will come, or they will bring some special toy or book, but they do not. And then, again, there is the problem of parents who, although they give presents and make clothes and do all sorts of things which of course are very important, just cannot give a hug at the right moment. Such parents may find it easier to love their child in the difficult conditions of a hospital ward. They come early and stay as long as possible, and bring more and more presents. After they have gone the child can hardly breathe. A girl once implored me (it was round about Christmas time), 'Take all those presents off the cot!' She was so weighed down by the burden of the expression of love which had taken this indirect form and had nothing to do with her mood.

It seems to me that the children of overbearing, unreliable, and highly excitable parents can get a great deal of relief for a while from being in hospital *unvisited*. The Sister of the ward has some children like this in her care, and we can see her point of view when she feels at times that *all* children are better unvisited. Also she is looking after the children whose parents live too far away to visit, and, most difficult of all, children who have no parents at all. Naturally, the visiting-hour does not help the Sister in the management of *these* children, who make special demands on her and the nurses because of their poor belief in human beings. For children with no good home a stay in hospital may provide the first good experience. Some of them do not even believe in human beings enough to be sad; they must make friends with any one who turns up, and when they are alone they rock backwards and forwards, or bang their heads on the pillow, or on the sides of the cot. You have no reason to let your child suffer on account of there being these deprived children in the ward, but at the same time you should know that the Sister's management of these less fortunate children can be made more difficult by the fact that other children are being visited by their own parents.

When all goes well, it may very likely be that the main effect of a stay in hospital is that afterwards the children have a new game; there was 'Fathers and Mothers', and then of course 'Schools', and now it is 'Doctors and Nurses'. Sometimes the victim is the baby, and sometimes it is a doll, a dog, or a cat.

The main thing I want to say is that the introduction of frequent visiting of children in hospital is an important step forward, and is in fact a reform long overdue. I welcome the new tendency as something which lessens distress and which, in the case of children of the toddler age, can easily make all the difference between good and thoroughly bad when a child must spend a certain length of time in hospital. I have drawn attention to the difficulties, which can be very real, because of the fact that I think that hospital visiting is so important.

Nowadays when we go into a children's ward we see a little child standing up in a cot, eager to find someone to talk to, and we may easily be greeted with these words, 'My mummy comes to see me!' This proud boast is a new phenomenon. And I can tell you about a little boy of three who was crying and the nurses were trying hard to find out how to make him happy. Cuddling was no good; he did not want it. At last they found that a certain chair had to be placed beside his cot. This calmed him down but it was some time before he could explain, 'That's for daddy to sit on when he comes to see me to-morrow'.

So you see, there must be something in this visiting business more than just preventing damage; but it is a good idea for parents to try to understand the difficulties so that the doctors and nurses will be able to keep up something which they know is good, but which they also know can spoil the quality of the very responsible work which they are doing for you.

9

On Adoption

[1955]

I WANT to support the accepted opinion that every adopted child should be told he or she is adopted, and should be told as early as possible, and told by the adoptive parents. You will want more than an opinion—you will want reasons. The main one is that somehow or other children find out in the course of time. How many times I have traced the cause of a change for the worse in a normal boy or girl to a remark overheard on the way to school, a child of a neighbour repeating what has been said 'above the child's head', so to speak, by grown-ups who did not know that their conversation was being listened to.

And it must be remembered that children lead full lives, meeting hate and vindictiveness as well as fun and games, and at some unpredictable moment the words come across in a nasty way that is intentional: 'You're not the child of your parents'. The nastiness would have been all right, that's just part of life, and it mixes up with the niceness; but for the adopted child the sting lies in the news, news which need not in itself have been nasty.

For it is not necessarily nasty to be an adopted child, as many of you know full well; yet it can be.

Very occasionally one has to agree to not telling a child about adoption; but the main thing is that the adopted child is practically certain to know eventually, and you have it in your power to give the news in the best possible way, and as early as possible.

How will you do it? I don't know exactly. You will find your own way, the way that suits your temperament. Often parents tell me that they have introduced a bed-time story, one of those that gets repeated endlessly, or that gets developed a little each night. This story somehow or other introduces the theme of an animal or a child that was lost and is found. These stories are popular with almost all small children, and all that is needed is for this type of story to be brought in with especial care and richness. The moment comes when you begin to indicate that this story has special application.

What about timing? I think the principle is that there is never an exactly right moment. At some point you crash in with your first remark : that's how it was with your Tim or Helen. You hold your breath, for you quite rightly feel the tremendous implication of your simple statement, but the chances are that it will seem to pass unnoticed. But what you have said is true, and therefore you somehow feel better. Gradually the pattern develops along true instead of false lines, and your little child grows up without that vulnerability that comes from the false situation.

You may find this very easy or very difficult. I can well understand if it is difficult, especially that first plunge. But I can assure you that the constant anxiety that belongs to deception is more wearing than the moment of panic that belongs to the first statement of truth.

The great merit of this story-telling method is that it leaves the way open for the question of whose tummy the child came out of. This question interests every child in a deep way, but the adopted child needs even more than your own child the truth about insides. I could say that your own child can afford to play about with gooseberry bushes, but not your adopted child. Moreover, a little later on, your adopted child will need further information about sex which your own child can acquire in a more haphazard way. I am talking about sex in animals and not in plants. Botany is not enough.

There is a reason why all this trouble can be worth while. You see, you are dealing with the child's mind. The more fundamental things have roots that go deeper than thinking things out; the little child knows *in a bodily way* that there was a state (which we call intra-uterine life, infant care, good enough mothering)—a state out of which he or she emerged as an individual. All that you are trying to do is to prevent the child from getting in a muddle *in the mind*. You are trying to give conditions that will enable the adopted child to join up all these body memories with thinking, imagination, understanding.

The word imagination takes me on to my next point. All children have ideas of being the offspring of parents other than their own—perhaps of the king and queen. Those ideas play a prominent part in the lives of some. These fantasies are valuable, and have no danger. They enter into the material of children's play, alongside the close and factual identifications with father and mother that characterise the game of 'fathers and mothers' or 'families'. In all this there is evidence of a developing sureness of ability to distinguish between fact and fantasy. The adopted child has a special task here, since the fantasy of other parents gets all mixed up with the fact that there are other parents (who are not available). Shall the real parents be facts, while you become a kind of living dream, or shall you be the hard fact while the imagination plays round the idea of the actual parents?

There is no answer to this question, except the answer given by your adopted child who is working out a way of life.

Adoptive parents have a need to be aware of what child development is about, much more so than parents who are caring for their own children. With their own children they can allow intuition full sway except when things go wrong and when a child is showing symptoms of illness. Adopted children need to be thought about, even when they are healthy.

An adolescent boy or girl may very naturally become interested in finding out all that can be found out about the real parents. I have helped adolescent children in this sort of research. It seems sometimes that if there are facts to be discovered, these must be discovered. If this happens to your adopted child I hope you will not feel insulted in any way. It is surely quite in the order of things for a human being to want to know about the beginning. In adolescence children begin to become interested in heredity, and especially there comes a need to know what could be said to the boy friend or the girl friend should the awkward question be asked. Behind all this there is the imagination tearing away at the vitals, while in the case of your own boy and girl the worst is known, and the best too.

The trouble is that it is not always possible to help a boy or girl in this research, not even possible to give the reasons why help cannot be given. We must expect our attitude in such cases to be infuriating and to produce uncomfortable reactions. Perhaps it is best that usually you genuinely don't know, and that is right. When we do know we can tell, and I do not believe that a good relationship existing between adopted children and their parents is disrupted by a successful research into facts.

Many of you can already boast that you have carried adoptions right through, and you are now perhaps grandparents. You may think that some of what I have said is unnecessarily complex. However, there are adoptive parents who have been disappointed, not so much because of the fact that things went wrong as because they were not told about the difficulties, or they expected the wrong things. If all went well, and you had no difficulties, all I can say is that you did better than you knew.

10

First Experiments in Independence

[1955]

PSYCHOLOGY is liable to be superficial and easy, or else deep and difficult. A curious thing about the study of the first activities of infants, and the objects they use when going to sleep or when apprehensive, is that these things seem to exist in a layer in between the superficial and the deep, in between the simple examination of obvious facts and a probing into the obscure realms of the unconscious. For this reason I want to draw attention to the use infants make of ordinary common objects, and to show that there is a great deal to be learned from observations which are commonly made, and from facts which are all the time on display.

I am talking about nothing more difficult than the ordinary normal child's teddy bear. Every one who has care of children has interesting details to give which are as characteristic in the case of each child as the other behaviour patterns, and which are never exactly the same in two cases.

At the beginning, as every one knows, infants mostly push their fists into their mouths, and very soon they are developing a pattern, perhaps choosing a certain finger, two fingers, or a thumb, for sucking, while with the other hand caressing some part of the mother or a bit of sheet, blanket, or wool, or perhaps their own hair. There are two things going on here; the first, with some part of the hand in the mouth, being clearly related to the excited feeding; the second is one stage further displaced from excitement, and is more nearly affectionate. Out of this affectionate fondling activity there can develop a relationship to something which happens to be lying around, and this object may become very important to the infant. In a sense this is the first possession, that is, the first thing in the world that belongs to the infant, and yet which is not part of the infant like the thumb, or the two fingers, or the mouth. How important this can be, therefore, is evidence of the beginning of a relationship to the world.

These things develop along with the beginning of a sense of security, and along with the beginnings of the infant's relationship to one person. They are evidence that things are going well in the child's emotional development, and that memories of relationships are beginning to be built up. These can be made use of again in this new relationship to the object, which I myself like to call a transitional object. It is not the object itself, of course, that is transitional; it represents the infant's transition from a state of being merged with the mother to a state of being in relation to the mother as something outside and separate.

Although I want to stress the health that is implied in these phenomena, I do not want to give the impression that something is necessarily wrong if an infant does not develop interests of the kind that I am describing. In some cases the mother herself is retained and needed in person by an infant, whereas another infant finds this so-called transitional object good enough and even perfect, provided the mother is there in the background. It is common, however, for an infant to become specifically attached to some object which soon acquires a name, and it is fun to look into the origin of the name, which often derives from some word that the infant has heard long before speech has become possible. Soon, of course, parents and relations present the infant with soft playthings which (perhaps for the sake of the grown-ups) are shaped like animals or babies. From the infant's point of view these shapes are not so important. It is more the texture and the smell which take on vital significance, and the smell is especially important, so that parents learn that these objects cannot be washed with impunity. Parents who are otherwise hygienic often find themselves forced to carry around a filthy smelly soft object simply for peace. The infant, now growing up a little, needs this to be available; needs it to be returned when thrown away over and over again from the cot and the pram; needs to be able to pull bits out of it, and to dribble over it. In fact, there is nothing that may not happen to this thing, which becomes subjected to a very primitive form of loving—a mixture of affectionate caressing and destructive attack. In time other objects are added, and these are more and more appropriately fashioned to resemble animals or babies. Moreover, as time goes on, the parents try to get the child to say 'ta', which means to acknowledge the fact that the doll or the teddy bear came from the world, and was not born out of the imagination of the infant.

If we go back to the first object, which may perhaps be a Harrington square, or a special woollen scarf, or the mother's handkerchief, we must admit, I believe, that from the infant's point of view it would be inappropriate for us to ask for the word 'ta', and the acknowledgment of the fact that the object came from the world. From the infant's point of view this first object was indeed created out of his or her imagination. It was the beginning of the infant's creation of the world, and it does seem that we have to admit that in the case of every infant the world has to be created anew. The world as it presents itself is of no meaning to the newly-developing human being unless it is created as well as discovered.

It is impossible to do justice to the enormous variety of the early possessions and techniques employed by infants at times of stress, and particularly at times of going to sleep.

Examples

A baby girl used her mother's rather long hair for caressing while thumb-sucking. When her own hair was long enough she pulled it—instead of her mother's—across her face, and sniffed at it, when she was going to sleep. She did this regularly until she was old enough to want to have her hair cut so as to be like a boy. She was pleased with the result until bed-time, when, of course, she became frantic. Fortunately, the parents had kept her hair, and a switch of it was given to her. Immediately she put it across her face in the ordinary way, sniffed at it, and went to sleep happily.

A boy baby became early interested in a coloured woollen covering. Before he was a year old he had become interested in sorting out the threads of wool that he had pulled out according to their colours. His interest in the texture of wool and in colours persisted, and in fact never left him, so that when he grew up he became a colour expert in a textile factory.

The value of the examples can only be that they illustrate the wide range of the phenomena and of the techniques employed by infants in health, at moments of stress and separation. Almost any one caring for children can supply examples, each one of which is fascinating to study, provided one first of all realises that every detail is important and significant. Sometimes, instead of objects we find techniques, like humming, or more hidden activities such as the matching of lights seen, or the study of the interplay of borders—as between two curtains that move slightly in the breeze, or the overlap of two objects that change in relation to each other according to movements of the infant's head. Sometimes thinking takes the place of visible activities.

Abnormalities. In order to stress the normality of these matters I would like to draw attention to the way in which separation can affect them. Roughly speaking, when the mother, or some other person on whom the infant is dependent, is absent, there is no immediate change, owing to the fact that the infant has an internal version of the mother which remains alive for a certain length of time. If the mother is away over a period of time which is beyond a certain limit, then the internal version fades; at the same time all these transitional phenomena become meaningless, and the infant is unable to make use of them. What we see now is an infant who must be nursed or fed, and who if left alone, tends to go over into exciting activities with sensuous gratification. What is lost is the whole intermediate area of affectionate contact. With the return of the mother, if the interval has not been too long, there first builds up a new internal version of her, and this takes time. The success of this re-establishment of confidence in the mother is shown by the return of the employment of intermediate activities. This which we see in infants becomes more obviously serious when at a later stage a child feels abandoned, and becomes unable to play, and unable to be affectionate or to accept affection. Along with this, as is well known, there can be compulsive erotic activities. The stealing of deprived children who are recovering can be said to be part of the search for the transitional object, which had been lost through the death or fading of the internalised version of the mother.

A baby girl always sucked a rough woollen cloth wrapped round her thumb. At 3 she was 'cured' of thumb-sucking by having the rag taken away. Later she developed a very severe compulsive nail-biting which accompanied compulsive reading at the time of going to sleep.

The nail-biting ceased when, at 11 years, she was helped to remember the woollen cloth, the pattern on it, and her love of it.

Evolution. In health there is an evolution from the transitional phenomenon, and the use of objects, to the whole play capacity of the child. It is very easy to see that playing is of vital importance to all children, and that the capacity for play is a sign of health in emotional development. I am trying to draw attention to the fact that an early version of this is the relationship of the infant to the first object. My hope is that if parents understand that these transitional objects are normal, and indeed signs of healthy growth, they will not feel ashamed when they find themselves carrying curious things about with them whenever they travel with their child. They will certainly not show disrespect for them, and they will do everything possible to avoid their loss. Like old soldiers these objects simply fade away. In other words they become the group of phenomena extending out into the whole of the realm of children's play, and of cultural activities and interests—that wide area which is intermediate between living in the external world and dreaming.

Evidently the task of sorting out external phenomena from dreams is a heavy one. It is a task that we all hope to be able to accomplish, so that we may claim to be sane. Nevertheless, we need a resting-place from this sorting-out, and we get it in our cultural interests and activities. For the little child we allow a wider area than we allow for ourselves in which imagination plays a dominant role, so that playing which makes use of the world, and yet retains all the intensity of the dream, is considered characteristic of the life of children. For the infant who is just starting on this terrible task of achieving adult sanity we allow an intermediate life, particularly at the time between waking and sleeping, and these phenomena that I am referring to, and the objects which are used, belong to the resting-place that we give to the infant at the beginning, when we only very slightly expect the sorting out of the dream from the real.

As a child psychiatrist, when I get into contact with children and find them drawing pictures, and talking about themselves and their dreams, I find to my surprise that they easily remember these very early objects. Often they surprise their parents by remembering bits of cloth and weird objects which the parents had long forgotten. If an object is still available, it is the child who knows just where, in the limbo of half-forgotten things, this thing still lies, perhaps right at the back of a bottom drawer, or up on the top shelf of a cupboard. It is distressing for children not only when the object is lost, as happens sometimes by accident, but also when some parent with a lack of understanding of its real significance gives it away to another baby. Some parents are so used to the idea of these objects that, as soon as a baby is born, they take the transitional object of the family, and tuck it up with the baby, expecting that it will have the same effect on the new baby as it had on the last one. Naturally, they may be disappointed, because the object turning up in this way may or may not come to have significance for the new infant. It all depends. It can readily be seen that to present an object in this way has its dangers, since, in a sense, it robs the new infant of the opportunity for creating. Certainly it is often very helpful when a child can make use of some object in the home; something that can be given a name, and that often becomes almost part of the family. Out of the infant's interest in this comes his eventual preoccupation with dolls, other toys, and animals.

This whole subject is a fascinating one for parents to study. They need not be psychologists in order to get a great deal of profit from watching, and perhaps recording, a line of development of such attachments and techniques in this intermediate area characteristic of each of their infants in turn.

11

Support for Normal Parents

[1944]

IF you have read as far as this you will have seen that I have tried to say something positive. I have not shown how difficulties can be overcome, or what ought to be done when children show signs of anxiety, or when parents quarrel in front of their children, but I have tried to give a little support to the sound instincts of normal parents, those who are likely to achieve and maintain a family of ordinary healthy children. There is much more to be said, but here is my attempt at a start.

It may be asked: Why trouble to talk to people who are doing well? surely the greater need comes from those parents who are in difficulties? Well, I try not to be weighed down by the fact that much distress undoubtedly exists even here in England, in London, in the district immediately around the hospital where I work. I know only too well about this distress, and about the anxiety and depression that prevail. But my hopes are based on the stable and healthy families which I also see building up around me, families that form the only basis for the stability of our society for the next couple of decades.

It may also be asked: Why concern yourself with healthy families which you say exist, and on which you base your hopes? Can they not manage for themselves? Well, I have a very good reason for giving active support here, which is this: there exist tendencies towards destruction of these good things. It is by no means wise to assume that what is good is safe from attack; rather is it true to say that the best always has to be defended if it is to survive discovery. There is always hate of what is good, and fear of it, unconscious chiefly, and liable to appear in the form of interferences, petty regulations, legal restrictions, and all manner of stupidities.

I do not mean that parents are ordered about or cramped by official policy. The State in England takes pains to leave parents free to choose, and to accept and to refuse what the State offers. Of course, births and deaths have to be registered, certain infectious diseases are notifiable, and children must attend school from 5 to 15. And boys and girls who break the law of the land come, with their parents, under some form of compulsion. However, the State provides a very large number of services which parents may make use of or may eschew. To mention a few, there are the nursery schools, vaccination against smallpox, immunisation against diphtheria, ante-natal and infant welfare clinics, cod-liver oil and fruit juices, dental treatment, cheap milk for infants and school milk for the older children; all these are available yet not compulsory. All of which suggests that the State in England to-day does recognise the fact that a good mother is the right judge of what is good for her own child, provided she is informed as to facts and educated as to needs.

The trouble is that those who actually administer these public services are by no means uniformly confident in the mother's ability to understand her child better than any one else can. Doctors and nurses are often so impressed with the ignorance and stupidity of some of the parents that they fail to allow for the wisdom of the others. Or perhaps the lack of confidence in mothers that is so often to be noted arises out of the specialised training of the doctors and nurses, who have expert knowledge of the body in sickness and in health, but who are not necessarily qualified to understand the parents' whole task. How easy for them to think, when a mother boggles at their expert advice, that she is doing so out of cussedness, when really she knows that it would harm her baby to be away from her in hospital at the moment he is being weaned, or that her boy ought to be able to understand more of what the world is like before he is whisked into hospital for circumcision, or that her girl is actually the wrong type for injections and immunisations (unless there is actually an epidemic) because of extreme nervousness.

What is a mother to do if she is worried by the doctor's decision that her child's tonsils should be removed? The doctor certainly knows about tonsils, but often he fails to impress the mother that he really understands how serious it is to take a child who feels well at the time and to operate on him when he is too young to have the matter explained to him. The mother can only stick up for her belief in the necessity of avoiding such an event if possible, and if she really believes in her instinct because she is educated in this matter of her child's developing personality, she can put her point of view to the doctor and play her part in coming to a decision. A doctor who respects the specialised knowledge of the parent easily wins respect for his own specialised knowledge.

Parents easily know that their own little children need to be provided with a simplified environment, and that they need this simplified environment until they are able to understand the significance of complications, and are therefore able to allow for these. There comes a time when the son and heir can have his tonsils out, if they really need removal, without harm to his personality development, and he may even find interest and pleasure in his hospital experience, and make a step forward through having been over the top, so to speak. But this time depends on the kind of child the boy is, not only on his age; and only one intimate with him as his mother is can judge, though to be sure a doctor ought to be able to help her think it all out.

The State is indeed wise in its policy of education of parents with non-compulsion, and the next step is education of those who administer the public services, and the deepening of their respect for the ordinary mother's feelings and instinctual knowledge regarding her own children. She is a specialist in this matter of her own children, and, if she is not over-awed by the voice of authority, she can be found to know well what is good and what is bad in the matter of management.

Whatever does not specifically back up the idea that parents are responsible people will in the long run be harmful to the very core of society.

What is significant is the individual's experience of developing from an infant into a child and an adolescent, in a family that continues to exist, and that considers itself capable of coping with its own localised problems—the problems of the world in miniature. In miniature, yes . . . but not smaller in regard to intensity of feelings and richness of experience, smaller only in the relatively unimportant sense of quantity of complexity.

If what I have written does no more than stimulate others to do better what I am doing here, to support ordinary people, and to give them the real and right reasons for their good instinctual feelings, then I shall be satisfied. Let us do all we can as doctors and nurses for the sick both in body and mind, and let the State do all it can for those who for one reason or another are left stranded, and need care and protection. But let us also remember that there are, fortunately, some normal men and women, especially among the less sophisticated members of the community, who are not afraid of feelings, and whose feelings we need not fear. To bring out the best in parents, we must leave them full responsibility with regard to what is their own affair, the upbringing of their own family.

POSTSCRIPT

The Mother's Contribution to Society

I SUPPOSE that every one has a paramount interest, a deep, driving propulsion towards something. If one's life lasts long enough, so that looking back becomes allowable, one discerns an urgent tendency that has integrated all the various and varied activities of one's private life, and one's professional career.

As for me, I can already see what a big part has been played in my work by the urge to find and to appreciate the ordinary good mother. Fathers, I know, are just as important, and indeed an interest in mothering includes an interest in fathers, and in the vital part they play in child care. But for me it has been to mothers that I have so deeply needed to speak.

It seems to me that there is something missing in human society. Children grow up and become in their turn fathers and mothers, but on the whole they do not grow up to know and acknowledge just what their mothers did for them at the start. The reason is that the part the mother plays has only recently begun to be perceived. But here I must make something clear; there are certain things I do not mean.

I do not mean that children should thank their parents for conceiving them. Surely they may hope that the original coming together was a matter of mutual pleasure and satisfaction. Parents certainly cannot expect thanks for the fact of a child's existence. Babies do not ask to be born.

There are other things I do not mean. For instance, I do not mean that children are under any obligation to their fathers and mothers at all on account of their co-operation in home-building and family affairs, even although gratitude may eventually develop. Ordinary good parents do build a home and stick together, thus providing the basic ration of child care and thus maintaining a setting in which each child can gradually find the self and the world, and a working relationship between the two. But parents do not want gratitude for this; they get their rewards, and rather than be thanked they prefer to see their children growing up and themselves becoming parents and home-builders. This can be put the other way round. Boys and girls can legitimately blame parents when, after bringing about their existence, they do not furnish them with that start in life which is their due.

In the last half century there has been a great increase in awareness of the value of the home. (It cannot be helped if this awareness came first out of an understanding of the effect of the bad home.) We know something of the reasons why this long and exacting task, the parents' job of seeing their children through, is a job worth doing; and in fact we believe that it provides the only real basis for society, and the only factory for the democratic tendency in a country's social system.

But the home is the parents', not the child's, responsibility. I want to be very clear that I am not asking any one to be expressing gratitude. What particularly concerns me neither goes back so far as conception nor is it as far forward as home-building. I am concerned with the mother's relation to her baby just before the birth and in the first weeks and months after the birth. I am trying to draw attention to the immense contribution to the individual and to society which the ordinary good mother with her husband in support makes at the beginning, and which she does *simply through being devoted to her infant.*

Is not this contribution of the devoted mother unrecognised precisely because it is immense? If this contribution is accepted it follows that every man or woman who is sane, every man or woman who feels to be a person in the world, and for whom the world means something, every happy person, is in infinite debt to a woman. At a time when as an infant (male or female) this person knew nothing about dependence, there was absolute dependence.

Once again, let me emphasise, the result of such recognition when it comes will not be gratitude or even praise. The result will be a lessening in ourselves of a fear. If our society delays making full acknowledgment of this dependence which is an historical fact in the initial stage of development of every individual, there must remain a block both to progress and to regression, a block that is based on fear. If there is no true recognition of the mother's part, then there must remain a vague fear of dependence. This fear will sometimes take the form of a fear of woman, or fear of a woman, and at other times will take less easily recognised forms, always including the fear of domination.

Unfortunately the fear of domination does not lead groups of people to avoid being dominated; on the contrary it draws them towards a specific or chosen domination. Indeed, were the psychology of the dictator studied one would expect to find that, amongst other things, he in his own personal struggle is trying to control the woman whose domination he unconsciously fears, trying to control her by encompassing her, acting for her, and in turn demanding total subjection and 'love'.

Many students of social history have thought that fear of woman is a powerful cause of the seemingly illogical behaviour of human beings in groups, but this fear is seldom traced to its root. Traced to its root in the history of each individual, this fear of woman turns out to be a fear of recognising the fact of dependence. There are therefore good social reasons for instigating research into the very early stages of the infant-mother relationship.

For my part, I happen to have been drawn towards finding out all I can about the meaning of the word devotion, and towards being able, if possible, to make a fully informed and fully felt acknowledgment to my own mother. Here a man is in a more difficult position than is a woman; he obviously cannot come to terms with his mother by becoming a mother, in turn, and in due course. He has no alternative but to go as far as he can towards a consciousness of the mother's achievement. The development of motherliness as a quality in his character does not get far enough, and femininity in a man proves to be a side-track to the main issues.

One solution for a man caught up in this problem is to take part in an objective study of the mother's part, especially the part she plays at the beginning.

At present the importance of the mother at the start is often denied, and instead it is said that in the early months it is only a technique of bodily care that is needed, and that therefore a good nurse will do just as well. We even find mothers (not I hope in this country) being told that they *must mother* their infants, this being the most extreme degree of denial that 'mothering' grows naturally out of being a mother. It often happens that just before an understanding of some matter, there is a stage of denial, or blindness, or deliberate not seeing, just as the sea withdraws from the sands before throwing forward the thundering wave.

Administrative tidiness, the dictates of hygiene, a laudable urge towards the promotion of bodily health, these and all sorts of other things get between the mother and her baby, and it is unlikely that mothers themselves will rise up in concerted effort to protest against interference. Someone must act for the young mothers who are having their first and second babies, and who are necessarily themselves in a dependent state. It can be assumed that no mother of a new-born baby will ever go on strike against doctors and nurses, however much frustration exists, because she is otherwise engaged.

The talks and essays in the first part of this book are mainly directed to mothers, but the young mothers who are chiefly concerned are unlikely to read them. I have no wish to alter this. I cannot assume that young mothers will ever want to know what it is that they do when they find they enjoy minding their own infants. They naturally fear lest instruction shall spoil their enjoyment and their creative experience, which is the essential element leading to satisfaction and growth. The young mother needs protection and information, and she needs the best that medical science can offer in the way of bodily care, and prevention of avoidable accidents. She needs a doctor and a nurse whom she knows, and in whom she has confidence. She also needs the devotion of a husband, and satisfying sexual experiences. No, the young mother is not usually a learner from books. Nevertheless, I have kept to the form of direct talk with young mothers for the reason that this provides a discipline. A writer on human nature needs to be constantly drawn towards simple English and away from the jargon of the psychologist, valuable as this jargon may be in contributions to scientific journals.

Probably some who have already been through the mothering experience, and who can therefore afford to have a look round, will be interested to read what is said in this way, and they may be able to help to do what is so much needed at the present time, that is to say, to give moral support to the ordinary good mother, educated or uneducated, clever or limited, rich or poor, and to protect her from every one and everything that gets between her baby and herself. We all join forces in enabling the emotional relationship between the mother and her new baby to start and to develop naturally. This collective task is an extension of the job of the father, of the father's job at the beginning, at the time when his wife is carrying, bearing, and suckling his infant; in the period before the infant can make use of him in other ways.

INDEX